Better Homes and Gardens®

Cajun Cooking

Our seal assures you that every recipe in *Cajun Cooking*
has been tested in the Better Homes and Gardens® Test Kitchen.
This means that each recipe is practical and reliable,
and meets our high standards of taste appeal.

BETTER HOMES AND GARDENS® BOOKS

Editor: Gerald M. Knox
Art Director: Ernest Shelton
Managing Editor: David A. Kirchner
Editorial Project Managers: James D. Blume, Marsha Jahns,
    Rosanne Weber Mattson, Mary Helen Schiltz

Department Head, Cook Books: Sharyl Heiken
Associate Department Heads: Sandra Granseth,
    Rosemary C. Hutchinson, Elizabeth Woolever
Senior Food Editors: Julia Malloy, Marcia Stanley,
    Joyce Trollope
Associate Food Editors: Linda Henry, Mary Major,
    Diana McMillen, Mary Jo Plutt, Maureen Powers,
    Martha Schiel, Linda Foley Woodrum
Test Kitchen: Director, Sharon Stilwell
    Photo Studio Director, Janet Pittman
    Home Economists: Lynn Blanchard, Jean Brekke, Kay Cargill,
    Marilyn Cornelius, Jennifer Darling, Maryellyn Krantz,
    Lynelle Munn, Dianna Nolin, Marge Steenson

Associate Art Directors: Linda Ford Vermie, Neoma Alt West,
    Randall Yontz
Assistant Art Directors: Lynda Haupert, Harijs Priekulis,
    Tom Wegner
Senior Graphic Designers: Jack Murphy, Stan Sams,
    Darla Whipple-Frain
Graphic Designers: Mike Burns, Sally Cooper, Blake Welch,
    Brian Wignall
Art Production: Director, John Berg; Associate, Joe Heuer;
    Office Manager, Emma Rediger

President, Book Group: Fred Stines
Vice President, Retail Marketing: Jamie Martin
Vice President, Direct Marketing: Arthur Heydendael

BETTER HOMES AND GARDENS® MAGAZINE
Vice President, Editorial Director: Doris Eby
Executive Director, Editorial Services: Duane L. Gregg
Food and Nutrition Editor: Nancy Byal

CAJUN COOKING

Editors: Mary Major, Diana McMillen
Consultant: Sandra Day
Editorial Project Manager: Rosanne Weber Mattson
Graphic Designer: Brian Wignall
Electronic Text Processor: Paula Forest
Contributing Photographers: Mike Dieter, M. Jensen
    Photography, Inc.
Food Stylists: Janet Pittman, Judy Tills
Contributing Illustrator: Thomas Rosborough

On the cover: *Seafood Gumbo* (see recipe, page 28)

Contents

4 Welcome to Cajun Country
A peek at southern Louisiana cooking.

6 The Basics: Roux
The flavorful beginning of many a dish.

8 Cajun Mainstays
Traditional favorites such as jambalaya,
courtbouillon, and sauce piquante.

24 Gumbo
A gumbo for every pot.

30 Crawfish Is King
The crowning glory of Acadiana.

36 Crab Boil
A Cajun picnic.

40 Fry It!
Crisp, crunchy seafood and more.

50 A Taste of the Bayou
What's what in Cajun ingredients.

56 Grits and More
A hearty hodgepodge of side dishes.

65 Pralines, Pig's Ears, and Pie
Cajun-style sweets.

76 Fais-Do-Do
A tradition of food, fun, and frolic.

82 Fresh from New Orleans
The best of New Orleans, à la carte.

95 Index

Welcome to Cajun Country

Cajun (KAY-jun) is one of the hottest cuisines around—both in popularity and spiciness.

It blends the recipes of early Acadian (French-Canadian) settlers, with a cupful of fresh Southern ingredients, and dashes of Creole, Italian, African and Southern cooking. Gumbo, redfish, okra, crawfish and jambalaya—they're all Cajun country favorites. Turn the page and discover the unique flavors for yourself.

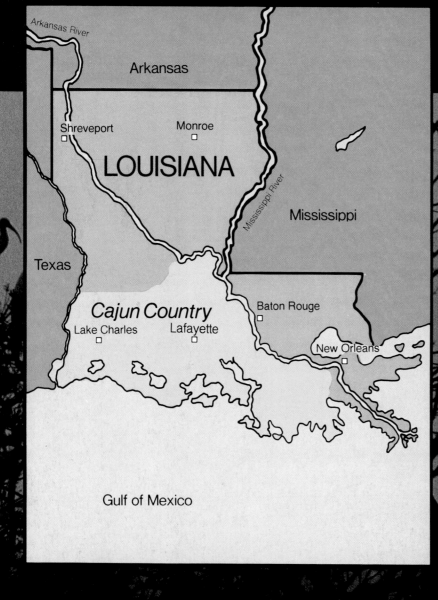

Roux

½ cup all-purpose flour
½ cup cooking oil

● In a heavy skillet or 2-quart saucepan stir together flour and cooking oil till smooth (see photo 1). Cook over medium-high heat for 5 minutes. Reduce heat to medium. Cook and stir about 10 minutes more or till a reddish brown roux is formed (see photo 2).

● **Dark Roux:** Prepare the Roux as directed, *except* cook and stir over medium heat about 15 minutes instead of 10 minutes or till a dark, reddish brown roux is formed (see photo 3).

● **Make-Ahead Roux:** Prepare the Roux or Dark Roux as directed. Cool and transfer to a tightly covered container. Store in the refrigerator for up to 2 weeks or freeze for 6 months. To use, heat in a covered saucepan.

Many basic Cajun dishes owe their color and rich flavor to a roux (roo). How do you make a roux? Mix a little cooking oil and some flour, then cook and stir and stir and stir. To be safe, cook in a heavy pan and stir with a long-handled wooden spoon. The slow cooking pays off. As the roux mixture cooks, it gets toastier in color and flavor.

1 Begin a roux by stirring together the flour and cooking oil, as shown. Then cook for 5 minutes over-medium-high heat.

2 Reduce the heat to medium so you can better control the cooking. For a light roux, heat about 10 minutes more. Stop cooking when your roux is reddish brown, as shown. Use this mildly flavored roux for fish and seafood dishes.

3 For a dark roux, cook on medium about 15 minutes. Here's what your roux should look like. Use this darker version for more robust meat and poultry dishes.

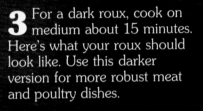

Redfish Courtbouillon

1 2- to 2½-pound fresh *or* frozen dressed redfish, *or* red snapper (with head and tail)

● Thaw fish, if frozen.

Cajuns prepare native Louisiana redfish in many different ways, but Courtbouillon (COO-bee-yon) is one of the best.

¼ cup all-purpose flour
¼ cup cooking oil

● In a heavy 3-quart saucepan stir together flour and oil till smooth. Cook over medium-high heat for 5 minutes, stirring constantly. Reduce heat to medium. Cook and stir about 10 minutes more or till a reddish brown roux is formed. (See pages 6-7.)

Outside of Louisiana, other fish are sometimes sold as redfish. To be sure you have the real thing, look for the telltale dark dot on the tail (see photo).

¾ cup chopped onion
¾ cup chopped green pepper
¾ cup chopped celery
2 cloves garlic, minced

● Add the onion, green pepper, celery, and garlic. Cook and stir for 5 minutes.

1 10½-ounce can tomato
 puree
1 8-ounce can tomatoes,
 cut up
½ teaspoon salt
2 bay leaves
¼ to ½ teaspoon ground red
 pepper

● Stir in, tomato puree, *undrained* tomatoes, salt, bay leaves, ground red pepper and 1¼ cups *water*. Bring to boiling. Reduce the heat. Simmer, uncovered, for 30 minutes.

⅓ cup dry wine
3 thin lemon slices
2 tablespoons snipped
 parsley
 Hot cooked rice

● Stir in wine, lemon, and parsley. Pour into poacher pan or roasting pan. Bring to boiling. Add fish. Cover and simmer for 25 to 30 minutes or till fish flakes. Remove bay leaves. Serve with rice. Garnish with additional lemon and bay leaves, if desired. Serves 6.

CUBED FISH VARIATION

Prepare Redfish Courtbouillon as directed, *except* use 1½ pounds fresh or frozen *redfish* or *red snapper fillets,* thawed and cubed. After stirring the wine, lemon, and parsley into the sauce, stir in the cubed fish. Cover and simmer for 2 to 3 minutes or till fish flakes easily with a fork. Serve over cooked rice. Makes 6 servings.

Blackened Redfish

1 1- to 1¼-pound fresh *or* frozen redfish *or* red snapper fillet, cut into 4 portions, *or* four 4-ounce fillets	● Thaw fish, if frozen.	**Watch out for the smoke! You can count on this dish really smoking up your kitchen. If you don't have an exhaust fan over your range, stick to the grill method.**
½ teaspoon onion powder ½ teaspoon garlic powder ½ teaspoon ground white pepper ½ teaspoon ground red pepper ½ teaspoon ground black pepper ½ teaspoon dried thyme, crushed ¼ teaspoon salt	● In a small bowl combine onion powder, garlic powder, white pepper, red pepper, black pepper, thyme, and salt.	
3 tablespoons butter *or* margarine, melted	● Heat a 12-inch iron skillet or heavy aluminum skillet over high heat. Meanwhile, brush fillets with some of the melted butter or margarine. Coat fillets on both sides with seasoning mixture.	
	● Add coated fillets to *unoiled* skillet. Drizzle a little remaining melted butter or margarine over each fillet. Cook, uncovered, over high heat about 2 minutes (3 minutes for 1-inch-thick portions) or till blackened. Turn. Drizzle with butter and cook for 1½ to 2 minutes or till blackened and fish flakes with a fork. Remove thinner fillets. Continue cooking thick portions for 1 to 3 minutes more or till done. Serves 4.	
	Grilling method: Coat fish with seasoning mixture as directed. Remove grill rack. Place the unoiled 12-inch skillet *directly atop hot* coals. Heat about 5 minutes or till drop of water sizzles. Add fish to skillet. Drizzle fillets with butter. Cook for 2½ to 3 minutes or till blackened. Turn. Drizzle with butter and cook for 2½ to 3 minutes or till blackened and fish flakes with a fork. Remove thinner fillets. Continue cooking thick portions for 1 to 2 minutes more. Makes 4 servings.	

Stuffed Pork Roast

⅓ cup finely chopped onion ⅓ cup finely chopped green pepper 2 cloves garlic, minced 1 teaspoon salt 1 teaspoon ground red pepper 1 teaspoon ground black pepper	● For stuffing, in a mixing bowl combine onion, green pepper, garlic, salt, red pepper, and black pepper. Mix well.
1 3- to 4-pound boneless pork loin roast	● Cut 12 to 14 deep slits, 1 inch wide, randomly around the pork roast. Using your fingers, stuff the slits with some of the stuffing. Place roast, fat side up, on a rack in a shallow roasting pan. Rub remaining stuffing mixture over roast. Insert a meat thermometer. (Make sure the bulb does not touch stuffing.)
	● Roast pork, uncovered, in a 325° oven for 2½ to 3 hours or till the meat thermometer registers 170°. Let pork roast stand about 15 minutes before carving. Makes 8 to 10 servings.

Pork is a Cajun staple because hogs thrive in the Louisiana marshes. So it's natural that stuffed pork roasts like this one are Sunday dinner favorites.

White Bean Soup

8 ounces dry great northern beans Water	● Rinse beans. In a 4-quart Dutch oven or kettle cover beans with water. Bring to boiling. Reduce heat. Simmer beans, uncovered, for 2 minutes. Remove from heat. Cover beans and let stand 1 hour. (Or, in a covered pan soak beans in water overnight in a cool place.) Drain beans and rinse.	Ham and hot pepper sauce jazz up the flavor of this colorful bean and tomato soup.
5 cups water 1 16-ounce can tomatoes, cut up ½ pound meaty ham bone *or* smoked pork hock 1 large onion, chopped ½ cup chopped green pepper ½ cup chopped celery 2 cloves garlic, minced ¼ teaspoon ground black pepper	● In the same Dutch oven combine beans, water, *undrained* tomatoes, ham bone, onion, green pepper, celery, garlic, and pepper. Bring to boiling. Reduce heat. Cover and simmer about 3 hours or till beans are tender. Remove ham bone. When cool enough to handle, cut meat from bone. Return meat to soup. Heat through.	
¼ teaspoon bottled hot pepper sauce Salt	● Stir in hot pepper sauce. Season to taste with salt. Makes 6 servings.	
	● **Note:** Freeze any leftover soup in individual servings in moisture- and vaporproof containers. To reheat, place frozen soup in a small saucepan. Reheat over medium-low heat, stirring soup occasionally, about 20 minutes.	

Pot-Roasted Rabbit

3 slices bacon	● In a 10-inch skillet cook bacon till crisp. Drain on paper towels, reserving bacon drippings in skillet. Crumble cooked bacon and set aside.
1 1½- to 2-pound domestic rabbit, cut up **Ground red pepper** **Ground black pepper** **1 cup all-purpose flour**	● Season rabbit with red and black peppers. Coat with flour. Brown rabbit in bacon drippings in skillet over medium heat. Remove rabbit from skillet.
4 ounces fresh mushrooms, sliced (1½ cups) **1 small onion, chopped** **¼ cup chopped green pepper** **2 cloves garlic, minced**	● Reserve *3 tablespoons* drippings in skillet. Add mushrooms, onion, green pepper, and garlic to reserved drippings. Cook about 5 minutes or till tender, stirring occasionally.
½ cup chicken broth **1 teaspoon Worcestershire sauce** **½ teaspoon dry mustard**	● Stir chicken broth, Worcestershire sauce, and dry mustard into vegetables in skillet. Add rabbit to skillet. Bring mixture to boiling. Cover and simmer about 45 minutes or till rabbit is tender.
	● Transfer rabbit to serving platter. Spoon fat off mixture in skillet. Spoon mixture over rabbit. Sprinkle with crumbled bacon. Makes 4 servings.

Rabbit, like other game, finds its way to many a Cajun meal. If you have wild rabbit, cook it as we do here, but simmer it a little longer until the meat is tender.

Chicken and Tasso Jambalaya

1 cup long-grain rice	● Cook rice according to package directions. Set aside.
1 large onion, chopped ½ cup chopped celery ½ cup chopped green pepper 2 cloves garlic, minced ¼ cup butter *or* margarine	● In a 3-quart saucepan cook onion, celery, green pepper, and garlic in butter or margarine till tender.
1 16-ounce can tomatoes, cut up ½ of a 6-ounce can (⅓ cup) tomato paste ½ cup chopped tasso *or* smoked sausage 1 teaspoon Creole seasoning *or* Three-Pepper Seasoning (see recipe, page 53)	● Stir in *undrained* tomatoes, tomato paste, tasso or sausage, and seasoning. Bring to boiling. Reduce heat. Cover and simmer 30 minutes.
2 whole chicken breasts (about 16 ounces each), skinned, boned, and cut into bite-size pieces ¼ teaspoon bottled hot pepper sauce	● Stir in chicken and hot pepper sauce. Simmer, covered, about 15 minutes more or till chicken is tender.
	● Stir in rice. Cook, stirring occasionally, till heated through. Makes 6 servings.

Spanish settlers also left their mark on Cajun cooking. Jambalaya (jam-ba-LIE-ya) is the Louisiana version of Spanish paella. The name comes from the French word, jambon, meaning ham. In our version, we used tasso (TAH-so), a spicy ham popular in Cajun country.

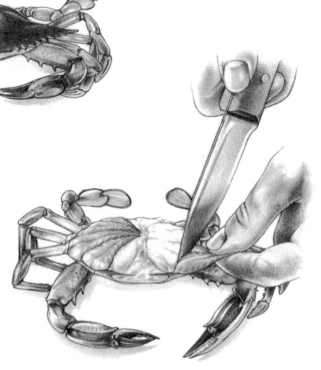

1 To cook hard-shell blue crabs, refer to the directions, opposite. Let the crabs cool slightly, then remove the meat. Hold the crab in your hand, back side down. Use your thumb to pry up the tail flap (apron), then twist off the flap and discard.

3 Use a small knife to trim the "devil's fingers" (spongy gills) from each side of the top of the crab, as shown. Discard the internal organs, the mouth, and the appendages at the front.

2 Hold the crab with the top shell in one hand and grasp the bottom shell where the apron was removed. Pull the top shell away from the body of the crab and set aside to use in the Stuffed Crab recipe, opposite.

4 Use your fingers to twist off the legs and claws. Discard the legs. Use a nutcracker to crack joints in the claws, then pick out the meat. Break the crab body in half and remove the meat.

Stuffed Crab

12 ounces cooked fresh *or* frozen crab meat	● Thaw crab meat, if frozen. Drain well. For fresh crab, remove meat as directed opposite, and save legs to use as a garnish, if desired.
1½ cups soft bread crumbs	● Spread crumbs in shallow baking pan. Bake in a 375° oven 6 to 8 minutes or till toasted, stirring occasionally.
1 medium onion, chopped (½ cup) **½ cup chopped celery** **¼ cup chopped green pepper** **¼ cup chopped green onions** **⅓ cup butter *or* margarine**	● In a medium saucepan cook onion, celery, green pepper, and green onions in butter or margarine over medium heat for 5 to 10 minutes or till tender. Remove from heat.
¼ cup snipped parsley **¼ teaspoon salt** **⅛ teaspoon ground red pepper** **⅛ teaspoon ground black pepper** **Lettuce leaves**	● Stir in crab meat, toasted bread crumbs, parsley, salt, red pepper, and black pepper. Spoon into 4 large or 8 small crab shells. (If you do not have shells, spoon into greased individual casseroles.) Arrange on baking sheet. Bake in a 375° oven for 10 to 15 minutes. Serve on lettuce and garnish with crab legs, if desired. Serves 4.

When buying live hard-shell blue crabs, count on one to three ounces of meat per crab. To cook them, bring 8 quarts water, 2 teaspoons salt, and if desired, some crab boil seasoning to a boil. Rinse 12 crabs in cold water and plunge into the boiling water. Return to boiling and cook 15 minutes. Drain and rinse the crabs under cold running water till cool. To remove the meat see illustrations, opposite.

Crab Chops

¼ cup butter *or* margarine ¼ cup all-purpose flour ½ teaspoon salt ¼ teaspoon ground red pepper 1 cup milk	● In a 2-quart saucepan melt butter or margarine. Stir in flour, salt, and red pepper. Add milk, stirring till blended. Cook and stir over medium heat till mixture is thickened and bubbly. Cook 1 minute more. Remove from heat.
12 ounces fresh *or* frozen crab meat ¼ cup finely chopped green onions	● Stir in crab meat and green onions. Chill for at least 2 hours or till mixture is firm enough to shape.
2¼ cups soft bread crumbs 2 beaten eggs	● Divide the mixture into 6 portions. Shape each portion into the shape of a pork chop, about ¾ inch thick. Carefully dip in crumbs to coat. Dip chops in beaten eggs, then dip in crumbs again. Chill 30 minutes to set the coating.
2 tablespoons butter *or* margarine	● In a 12-inch skillet melt butter or margarine over medium heat. Add crab chops and cook for 4 to 5 minutes on first side. If necessary, add another 1 to 2 tablespoons butter or margarine to prevent sticking. Turn chops carefully and cook for 4 to 5 minutes more or till golden brown. Makes 6 servings.

These may look like pork chops, but your tongue will tell you they're crab. The Catholic Cajuns often disguised fish and seafood to look like meat to serve on meatless Fridays.

Use the pattern below to help you shape the seafood chops.

Crab Chop Shape

Grillades

1 **pound pork tenderloin, cut into 3-inch strips**	● Using a meat mallet, pound meat to ¼-inch thickness. Combine flour and salt. Coat meat with the flour mixture.
¼ **cup all-purpose flour**	
¼ **teaspoon salt**	In a large skillet cook meat, half at a time, in hot oil for 2 to 4 minutes or till
1 **tablespoon cooking oil**	brown, turning once. Remove the meat from skillet.

1 **16-ounce can tomatoes, cut up**	● In the skillet stir together *undrained* tomatoes, onions, green onions, celery, parsley, garlic, and red and black pepper.
2 **medium onions, chopped**	Bring to boiling. Cover and simmer over low heat 20 minutes.
½ **cup chopped green onions**	
½ **cup chopped celery**	Add meat. Simmer, covered, for 5 to 10 minutes more. Serve over hot cooked
2 **tablespoons snipped parsley**	rice or grits. Makes 4 servings.
2 **cloves garlic, minced**	
⅛ **teaspoon ground red pepper**	
⅛ **teaspoon ground black pepper**	
Hot cooked rice *or* grits	

Southerners like hearty breakfasts such as Grillades (gree-ODDS) with grits.

Sausage-Stuffed Duck

¼ **pound andouille *or* smoked sausage, cut into ½-inch cubes**	● In a medium saucepan cook andouille or sausage, celery, apple, onion, and red pepper in butter or margarine till the vegetables are tender. Remove from heat.
½ **cup finely chopped celery**	Place croutons in a large mixing bowl.
½ **cup finely chopped apple**	Sprinkle with onion mixture and broth.
¼ **cup finely chopped onion**	Toss lightly till well mixed. Set aside.
¼ **teaspoon ground red pepper**	
2 **tablespoons butter *or* margarine**	
4 **cups plain croutons**	
¼ **cup chicken broth**	

1 **4- to 5-pound domestic duckling**	● Rinse duck and pat dry with paper towels. Sprinkle inside of cavity with salt.
Salt	Spoon some of the stuffing into the neck cavity. Fasten the neck skin securely to the back of bird with a small skewer. Lightly spoon remaining stuffing into the body. Tie legs securely to the tail. Twist wing tips under back. Prick skin all over with a fork. Place duckling, breast side up, on a rack in a shallow roasting pan.
	Roast, uncovered, in a 375° oven for 1¾ to 2¼ hours or till a meat thermometer registers 180° to 185°. Spoon off fat during roasting. Cover and let stand 15 minutes before carving. Makes 6 servings.

Most Cajuns would use a wild duck, but we chose the more readily available domestic variety. The sausage and apple filling gives either type of duck a smoky, sweet flavor.

Baked Flounder with Shrimp-and-Crab Stuffing

1½ cups soft bread crumbs
¼ cup butter *or* margarine

● In a 10-inch skillet cook bread crumbs in the butter or margarine over medium heat till golden brown and crisp. Remove crumbs to mixing bowl.

2 tablespoons butter *or* margarine
½ cup chopped green onions
½ cup chopped celery
½ cup chopped green pepper
2 cloves garlic, minced

● In the same skillet melt butter or margarine. Add green onions, celery, green pepper, and garlic. Cook over medium heat till vegetables are tender. Add vegetables to bread crumbs.

8 ounces fresh *or* frozen shrimp, cooked, shelled, and coarsely chopped
6 to 8 ounces fresh crab meat *or* frozen crab meat, thawed
2 tablespoons snipped parsley
¼ teaspoon salt
¼ teaspoon ground red pepper
¼ teaspoon ground black pepper

● Stir chopped shrimp, crab meat, parsley, salt, red pepper, and black pepper into bread mixture.

2 1- to 1¼-pound dressed flounder (with head and tail)

● Rinse fish and pat dry. To cut a pocket, place flounder on a board, dark side up. Make a slit in the center of fish, cutting lengthwise along backbone (see photo 1, right). Cut a pocket on both sides of first cut.

2 tablespoons butter *or* margarine, melted
Lime slices (optional)
Green onion (optional)

● Stuff fish loosely with bread mixture (see photo 2, right). Place fish in a greased 15½x10½x2-inch baking dish. Brush fish with butter. Bake in a 400° oven about 20 minutes or till fish flakes easily with a fork. Transfer fish to a serving platter. Garnish the cooked fish with lime slices and green onion, if desired. Makes 4 servings.

To serve stuffed flounder, cut crosswise across the top of the fish and stuffing to the backbone. Then, holding the knife horizontally, cut around outside edge of fish. With a spatula, lift off the meat and stuffing.

To remove backbone, slide a knife under backbone, starting at tail, and lift it away from fish. Use a fork to help lift bone. Cut fish into serving-size pieces and serve with stuffing.

1 To stuff the fish, use a sharp knife to cut along the line on the fish's dark side. Make a 5- to 6-inch slit.

2 With the knife blade parallel to the ribs, cut a pocket in the fish on both sides of the slit. Stuff loosely with the bread mixture.

Sauce Piquante

1½ pounds fresh *or* frozen redfish, red snapper, *or* catfish fillets *or* Peppered Pork Chops (see recipe, right)	● Thaw fish, if frozen. Cut the fillets into 1-inch pieces.
½ cup all-purpose flour ½ cup cooking oil	● In a heavy 4-quart Dutch oven stir together flour and oil till smooth. Cook over medium-high heat for 5 minutes, stirring constantly. Reduce heat to medium. Cook and stir about 10 minutes more or till a reddish-brown roux forms. (See pages 6-7.)
2 large onions, chopped (1½ cups) 1 cup chopped green pepper 1 cup chopped celery 2 cloves garlic, minced	● Stir in onions, green pepper, celery, and garlic. Cook and stir for 5 to 10 minutes or till vegetables are tender.
2 10-ounce cans tomatoes and green chili peppers 2 8-ounce cans tomato sauce 2 cups Fish Stock (see recipe, right) *or* chicken broth ½ teaspoon salt ¼ teaspoon ground black pepper ⅛ to ¼ teaspoon ground red pepper	● In a blender container place *undrained* tomatoes and green chili peppers. Cover and blend till smooth. Stir blended tomatoes, tomato sauce, Fish Stock or chicken broth, salt, black pepper, and red pepper into the Dutch oven. Simmer, uncovered, for 45 minutes to 1 hour or till thick.
Hot cooked rice	● For fish, stir in fish. Cook about 5 minutes more or till fish flakes easily with a fork. Serve with rice. For Peppered Pork Chops, serve sauce over chops with rice. Makes 6 servings.

Not every sauce has its day, but once a year the town of Raceland, Louisiana holds a Sauce Piquante festival. Celebrants gorge themselves on fish, seafood, poultry, and meat cooked in this peppery concoction.

Fish Stock:

Peppered Pork Chops

1½ teaspoons ground white pepper
1½ teaspoons ground red pepper
1½ teaspoons ground black pepper
 6 pork loin chops, cut ¾ to 1 inch thick

● Combine white pepper, red pepper, and black pepper. Rub each chop with about ¾ *teaspoon* of the pepper mixture. Place chops on the rack of an unheated broiler pan. Broil chops 3 to 4 inches from the heat for 20 to 25 minutes or till no pink remains, turning once. Serve with Sauce Piquante (see recipe, left), if desired. Makes 6 servings.

Good meat was scarce in early Louisiana. While this may have disheartened lesser folk, the resilient Cajuns formed local co-ops that provided each member with some kind of meat once a week.

Fish Stock

Fishing for compliments? For some sure-fire bait make Sauce Piquante and other fish dishes with Fish Stock.

In a 4-quart Dutch oven combine 1 pound *fish heads and tails;* 4 cups *water;* 1 large *onion,* chopped; 2 stalks *celery,* chopped; and ½ teaspoon *salt.* Bring to boiling. Reduce heat. Cover and simmer 30 minutes. Strain the stock through a sieve lined with cheesecloth. Makes about 2½ cups.

Chicken, Oyster, And Sausage Gumbo

⅓ cup all-purpose flour
⅓ cup cooking oil

● In a heavy 4-quart Dutch oven stir together the flour and oil till smooth. Cook over medium-high heat 5 minutes, stirring constantly. Reduce heat to medium. Cook and stir the roux constantly about 15 minutes more or till a dark reddish brown roux is formed. (See pages 6-7.)

The Choctaw Indians first ground dried sassafras leaves to make filé powder. But Cajun cooks popularized it when they added it to gumbo to thicken and to add a thyme-like flavor.

1 large onion, chopped
½ cup chopped green pepper
4 cloves garlic, minced
½ teaspoon ground black pepper
¼ teaspoon ground red pepper

● Stir in the onion, green pepper, garlic, black pepper, and red pepper. Cook and stir over medium heat for 3 to 5 minutes or till vegetables are tender.

Because filé powder becomes stringy when boiled, we suggest you add it to your gumbo just before serving, or let each person add his own.

4 cups hot water
2 pounds chicken thighs, skinned, boned, and cut into bite-size pieces

● Gradually stir the hot water into the vegetable mixture. Stir in chicken. Bring mixture to boiling. Reduce heat. Cover and simmer for 40 minutes.

12 ounces andouille *or* smoked sausage, cut into ½-inch slices and quartered

● Stir in the sausage. Cover and simmer about 20 minutes more or till chicken is tender. Remove from heat. Skim off fat.

1 pint shucked oysters
Hot cooked rice
Whole okra, split to stem (optional)
Filé powder (optional)

● Drain oysters and stir into gumbo. Cover and simmer for 5 to 10 minutes or till oysters are done and mixture is heated through.

Spoon over hot cooked rice and garnish with okra, if desired. Serve with ¼ to ½ teaspoon filé powder to the side of each serving to stir into gumbo, if desired. Makes 6 servings.

Green Gumbo

½ pound spinach (6 cups)
½ pound fresh collard
    greens, mustard greens,
    or kale, *or* one-10 ounce
    package frozen mustard
    greens *or* kale (6 cups)
1 bunch watercress (2 cups)
1 bunch parsley (2 cups)
1 cup shredded cabbage
⅓ cup water

● Wash all the greens thoroughly to remove sand. Drain well.

    In a 4-quart Dutch oven combine greens and water. Bring to boiling. Reduce heat. Cover and simmer for 12 to 15 minutes or till tender. Drain greens, reserving liquid. Cut up the cooked greens. Set aside.

It's a Cajun custom to make and serve *Green Gumbo* (known to some as gumbo z'herbes) without meat on Good Friday. Tradition said that in the coming year, you would make one new friend for each green you added to the pot.

½ cup all-purpose flour
½ cup cooking oil

● In a heavy 4-quart Dutch oven stir together the flour and oil till smooth. Cook over medium-high heat for 5 minutes, stirring constantly. Reduce heat to medium. Cook and stir about 10 minutes more or till a reddish brown roux is formed (See pages 6-7).

2 large onions, chopped
1 cup chopped green pepper
1 cup chopped celery

● Add onions, green pepper, and celery. Cook and stir over medium heat 5 to 10 minutes or till vegetables are very tender.

1¼ pounds fully cooked ham,
    cut into ½-inch cubes
¼ teaspoon salt
¼ teaspoon ground red
    pepper
¼ teaspoon ground black
    pepper
Hot cooked rice

● Add enough water to reserved cooking liquid to make 2 cups. Add water mixture, chopped greens, ham, salt, red pepper, and black pepper to onion mixture. Bring to boiling. Reduce heat. Cover and simmer about 1 hour. Serve over hot cooked rice. Serves 6.

Kale

Mustard greens

Collard greens

Seafood Gumbo

1 pound fresh *or* frozen shelled shrimp 6 to 8 ounces fresh *or* frozen crab meat	● Thaw shelled shrimp and crab meat, if frozen.
⅓ cup all-purpose flour ⅓ cup cooking oil	● In a 4-quart Dutch oven or large heavy saucepan stir together flour and cooking oil till smooth. Cook over medium-high heat 5 minutes, stirring constantly. Reduce heat to medium. Cook and stir constantly about 10 minutes more or till a reddish-brown roux forms. (See pages 6-7.)
2 large onions, chopped 1 large green pepper, chopped (1 cup) 6 cloves garlic, minced	● Add the onions, green pepper, and garlic. Cook and stir over medium heat about 10 minutes or till the vegetables are very tender.
2½ cups chicken broth *or* Shrimp Stock (see tip, page 35) 2 cups sliced okra *or* one 10-ounce package frozen cut okra, thawed ¾ teaspoon salt ¼ teaspoon ground red pepper ¼ teaspoon ground black pepper 2 bay leaves	● Gradually stir in chicken broth or Shrimp Stock, okra, salt, red pepper, black pepper, and bay leaves. Bring to boiling. Reduce heat. Cover and simmer about 30 minutes.
Hot cooked rice	● Add shrimp and crab meat. Simmer about 5 minutes or till the shrimp turn pink. Remove bay leaf. Season to taste. Serve over rice. Makes 6 servings.

The Cajuns invented gumbo when they tried to duplicate bouillabaise, the fish stew of France, using seafood and vegetables native to Louisiana.

Chicken and Okra Gumbo

1 2½- to 3-pound broiler-fryer chicken, cut up 1½ teaspoons salt ½ teaspoon ground black pepper ¼ to ½ teaspoon ground red pepper ½ cup cooking oil	● Sprinkle the chicken pieces with salt, black pepper, and red pepper. In a 4-quart Dutch oven brown chicken, half at a time, in hot cooking oil. Remove chicken and set aside. Reserve ½ cup drippings in Dutch oven.
½ cup all-purpose flour	● Add flour to pan drippings in Dutch oven, scraping bottom of pan to loosen drippings. Cook over medium-high heat 5 minutes, stirring constantly. Reduce heat to medium. Cook and stir about 15 minutes more or till a dark reddish-brown roux forms. (See pages 6-7.)
1 large onion, chopped 1 cup chopped green pepper 1 cup chopped celery 4 cloves garlic, minced	● Add onion, green pepper, celery, and garlic to the roux. Cook and stir over medium heat for 3 to 5 minutes or till vegetables are tender.
4 cups hot water	● Gradually stir the hot water into the vegetable mixture. Add chicken to the Dutch oven. Bring to boiling. Reduce heat. Cover and simmer about 1 hour or till chicken is very tender, adding more water, if necessary.
2 cups sliced okra *or* one 10-ounce package frozen cut okra, thawed 4 green onions, sliced ¼ cup snipped parsley Hot cooked rice	● Stir in okra, green onions, and parsley. Cover and simmer for 20 to 30 minutes more. Remove from heat. Skim off fat. Serve with rice. Makes 6 servings.

Anything goes in gumbo (an African word for okra). In Louisiana no two gumbos are exactly the same. The only gumbo-cooking rules are:
1. Start with a roux.
2. Thicken with either okra or filé powder.

Crawfish Ea

Live crawfish

Bayous offer Cajuns an important ingredient—crawfish. These shellfish look like miniature lobster and taste like shrimp, only sweeter.

Crawfish turn a bright red when they're cooked. To assure freshness, look for a curled tail. It means the crawfish was alive up until it was cooked. Discard those with straight tails.

Cooked crawfish

All the meat is in the tail. Plan 1 pound of crawfish per serving (3 to 4 ounces of meat). The real trick is getting that meat out. See our easy-to-follow instructions, opposite.

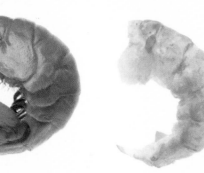

Crawfish tail with shell   Crawfish tail meat

ting Guide

1 To take the crawfish meat from the shell, gently twist the tail away from the body.

2 Unwrap the first 2 to 3 sections of shell on the tail to expose more meat.

3 Pinch the end of the tail and with your other hand, pull out the meat. If you like, dip the meat in Cocktail Sauce (see recipe, page 49).

4 For a Cajun-style finish, suck the flavorful juices from the head.

1 Roll out half of the pastry at a time to ⅛-inch thickness. For more even pastry, roll from the center to the edge.

Crawfish Pies

1 **pound fresh *or* frozen cooked, shelled, crawfish tails *or* shrimp** ¼ **cup butter *or* margarine** 1 **cup chopped onion** ½ **cup chopped green pepper** ½ **cup chopped celery** 4 **green onions with tops, chopped (½ cup)** 2 **tablespoons snipped parsley** 2 **cloves garlic, minced**	● Thaw crawfish or shrimp, if frozen. In a 3-quart saucepan melt butter or margarine. Add onion, green pepper, celery, green onions, parsley, and garlic. Cook and stir about 10 minutes or till vegetables are very tender.	**Whether you call them écrevisses, crawdads, creekcrabs, yabbies, mudbugs, or crawfish, they taste terrific in these main-dish pot pies.**

Whether you call them écrevisses, crawdads, creekcrabs, yabbies, mudbugs, or crawfish, they taste terrific in these main-dish pot pies.

¼ **cup all-purpose flour** 2 **cups chicken broth** ½ **of an 8-ounce can tomato sauce (about ½ cup)** ¼ **teaspoon salt** ⅛ **to ¼ teaspoon ground red pepper** ⅛ **to ¼ teaspoon ground black pepper**	● Stir in flour till blended. Stir in chicken broth, tomato sauce, salt, red pepper, and black pepper. Bring to boiling. Reduce heat. Cover and simmer mixture for 20 to 25 minutes.

---

2 **tablespoons cornstarch** 2 **tablespoons water**	● Combine cornstarch and water. Stir into skillet. Add crawfish. Cook and stir till thickened and bubbly. Cook 2 minutes more. Remove from heat.

Pastry (see recipe, right) **Milk**	● Prepare pastry. Roll out *half* of the pastry to ⅛-inch thickness. Cut 2 bottom crusts to fit 3 inches wider than a 10-ounce casserole (see inset photo, right). Ease 1 crust into each of 2 casseroles. Trim even with edge. Cut 2 top crusts 1 inch wider than casseroles. Pour 1 cup filling into each pastry-lined casserole. Top each with a pastry round. Fold extra pastry under bottom crust. Flute edge. Repeat to make 2 more pies. Cut decorative trimmings from pastry scraps and arrange on pies, if desired. Brush crusts with milk. Bake in a 425° oven for 20 to 25 minutes. Makes 4 servings.

PASTRY

In a large mixing bowl stir together 3 cups all-purpose *flour* and ¼ teaspoon *salt*. Cut in 1 cup *shortening* or *lard* till pieces are the size of small peas. Add 8 to 10 tablespoons *cold water,* 1 tablespoon at a time, tossing mixture with a fork till moistened. Divide pastry in half. Shape pastry into 2 balls.

2 Cut the bottom crust so it's 3 inches wider than the casserole. That allows room for the pastry to ease into the casserole dish.

3 Trim the pastry so it's about even with the edge of the casserole rim. Then, pour about one cup of filling into the pastry-lined casserole.

Crawfish Etouffée

1 pound fresh *or* frozen peeled crawfish tails *or* shrimp	● Thaw crawfish tails or shrimp, if frozen.	**Etouffée (AY-too-FAY) in Cajun cooking refers to simmering crawfish or shrimp "smothered" in onions, green pepper, celery, and tomato sauce.**
2 large onions, finely chopped (1½ cups) 1 cup finely chopped celery ½ cup finely chopped green pepper 2 cloves garlic, minced ¼ cup cooking oil, butter, *or* margarine	● In a heavy 3-quart saucepan cook onions, celery, green pepper, and garlic, covered, in oil, butter, or margarine about 10 minutes or till tender.	
2 tablespoons crawfish fat, butter, *or* margarine 4 teaspoons cornstarch	● Add crawfish fat, butter, or margarine, stirring till melted. Stir in cornstarch.	**The orange fat found in the heads of crawfish adds extra richness and flavor to dishes. Since it's difficult to find crawfish fat outside of Southern Louisiana, you'll probably want to substitute butter or margarine.**
1 cup water ½ cup tomato sauce ½ teaspoon salt ¼ to ½ teaspoon ground red pepper ¼ teaspoon ground black pepper Hot cooked rice	● Stir in crawfish or shrimp, water, tomato sauce, salt, red pepper, and black pepper. Bring mixture to boiling. Reduce heat. Simmer, uncovered, about 5 minutes or till crawfish are tender or shrimp turn pink. Serve with hot cooked rice. Makes 4 servings.	

Crawfish Stew

12 ounces fresh *or* frozen peeled crawfish tails *or* shrimp	● Thaw crawfish tails or shrimp, if frozen.
¼ cup all-purpose flour ¼ cup cooking oil	● In a heavy 2-quart saucepan stir together flour and oil till smooth. Cook over medium-high heat for 5 minutes, stirring constantly. Reduce heat to medium. Cook and stir about 10 minutes more or till a reddish-brown roux forms. (See pages 6-7.)
½ cup chopped onion ¼ cup chopped green pepper ¼ cup chopped celery	● Add onion, green pepper, and celery. Cook for 3 to 5 minutes or till tender.
2 cups Shrimp Stock (see tip, below) *or* chicken broth ½ teaspoon salt ¼ teaspoon ground black pepper ⅛ to ¼ teaspoon ground red pepper	● Add Shrimp Stock or chicken broth, salt, black pepper, and red pepper. Bring to boiling. Add crawfish or shrimp. Simmer, uncovered, for 1 to 3 minutes or till the crawfish are tender or the shrimp turn pink.
2 tablespoons crawfish fat (optional) Hot cooked rice	● Stir in crawfish fat, if desired. Serve over hot cooked rice. Makes 4 servings.

Crawfish and lobsters are country cousins. Crawfish look like tiny lobsters, but they live in fresh rather than salt water. Since Cajuns love them so much, they've taken to farming crawfish. Fresh crawfish are plentiful from March to June. Frozen crawfish tails are available year round.

Shrimp Stock

If you buy shrimp in the shell, don't throw away those shells! At least not yet. Instead, freeze them until you have enough to make a delicious homemade stock.

   To make stock, place the shells from 2 pounds *shrimp* in a large saucepan. Add 1 large *onion,* chopped; 2 small stalks *celery* with leaves, chopped; 4 sprigs *parsley;* 6 slices *lemon;* 1 teaspoon *salt;* 4 *whole black peppercorns;* and 4 *whole cloves.* Add 6 cups *cold water.* Bring to boiling over high heat. Reduce heat. Simmer 30 minutes. Strain through a cheesecloth-lined sieve. Discard shells, vegetables, lemon and spices. Makes about 6 cups.

Crab Boil

Cajuns call it a Crab Boil, but crawfish play a big part, too—along with potatoes and corn on the cob. They all simmer together for carefree cooking. For fun and for easy cleanup, serve them the traditional way, on newspapers. Then add French bread and beer. When the main course is over, bring on southern Pecan Pie (see recipes, pages 38–39).

Crab Boil!

THE MENU

Crab Boil

French Bread
(see recipe, page 78)

Pecan Pie

Beer or iced tea

MAKING IT HAPPEN

Several Hours Ahead:
- Make the Pecan Pie.
- Make French Bread.
- Prepare iced tea, if desired.
- Organize serving platters, plates, and utensils.

1 Hour Ahead:
- Heat water for Crab Boil.
- Cut up the vegetables for the boil.

25 Minutes Ahead:
- Prepare Crab Boil.
- Slice French bread.

At Serving Time:
- Arrange crabs, crawfish, and vegetables on serving platter.
- Pour the beer or iced tea.

Crab Boil

Pictured on pages 36-37.

10 quarts water
1 cup purchased *or* homemade crab boil seasoning (see recipe, page 53)
4 teaspoons salt

- In *each* of 2 very large pots bring *5 quarts* water, *½ cup* purchased or homemade crab boil seasoning, and *2 teaspoons* salt to boiling.

Take a tip from a Cajun cook. Before cooking crawfish soak them in salted water to reduce the size of the black vein that runs down the backs of the tails.

8 fresh ears of corn, halved
8 small potatoes, peeled and halved
4 small onions, halved
4 lemons, quartered

- Divide corn, potatoes, onions, and lemons between the 2 pots. Return to boiling. Reduce heat. Cover and simmer 10 minutes.

4 pounds live hard-shell blue crabs
4 pounds live crawfish

- Rinse crabs and crawfish in water. Add crabs to one pot of boiling water. Return to boiling. Reduce heat and simmer, covered, for 15 minutes.

   Add crawfish to the other pot. Return to boiling. Reduce heat and simmer, covered, 5 minutes.

   To serve, with a slotted spoon remove crabs, crawfish, corn, potatoes, and onions to a serving platter. Makes 8 servings.

Pecan Pie

Pastry for Single-Crust
  Pie (see recipe, below)

● Prepare and roll out pastry. Line a 9-inch pie plate with pastry. Trim pastry to ½ inch beyond edge of pie plate. Flute edge. *Do not prick pastry.*

The Cajuns can't take credit for Pecan Pie. But they CAN claim the good sense to include it in their recipe repertoire.

3 eggs
½ cup sugar
1 teaspoon vanilla
1 cup dark corn syrup
⅓ cup butter *or* margarine,
  melted
1½ cups coarsely chopped
  pecans

● In a mixing bowl beat eggs slightly. Beat in sugar and vanilla. Stir in corn syrup and melted butter or margarine. Mix well. Stir in pecans. Pour into prepared crust.

● To prevent overbrowning, cover edge of pie with foil. Bake in a 350° oven for 25 minutes. Remove foil. Bake about 20 minutes more or till a knife inserted off-center comes out clean.

  Cool on a wire rack. Cover and store in the refrigerator. Makes 8 servings.

Pastry for Single-Crust Pie: In a mixing bowl stir together 1¼ cups *all-purpose flour* and ¼ teaspoon *salt.* Cut in ⅓ cup *shortening or lard* till pieces are the size of small peas. Sprinkle 3 to 4 tablespoons *cold water* over the flour mixture, tossing gently with a fork till all is moistened. Form dough into a ball. Roll out as directed above.

1 To clean a soft-shell crab, hold the crab between the back legs. Using kitchen shears, remove the head by cutting horizontally across the body ½ inch behind the eyes.

2 Lift the pointed, soft top shell on one side to expose the "devil's fingers" (the spongy projectiles on the exposed side).

3 Using your fingers, push up the devil's fingers and pull off. Replace the soft top shell over the body. Repeat on the other side.

Fried Soft-Shell Crabs

4 large *or* 8 small soft-shell blue crabs	● To clean the soft-shell crabs, refer to photos, above.
1 beaten egg ¼ cup milk ½ cup all-purpose flour ¼ teaspoon salt ⅛ teaspoon ground red pepper	● In a shallow dish combine egg and milk. In another dish combine flour, salt, and red pepper. Dip crabs in egg mixture. Then roll in flour mixture.
Shortening *or* cooking oil for shallow-fat frying	● In an 8- or 10-inch skillet heat ½ inch melted shortening or cooking oil till hot. Add 2 or 3 of the crabs, back side down. Fry for 3 to 5 minutes or till golden. Turn carefully. Fry for 2 to 3 minutes more or till crabs are crisp and golden. Drain on paper towels. Keep crabs warm in a 300° oven. Repeat frying with the remaining crabs.
Kale (optional) Sliced kumquats (optional)	● To serve, garnish with kale and sliced kumquats, if desired. Makes 4 servings.

Soft-shell crab fanatics, mark your calendars! The buster crab season runs April through August. Busters are blue crabs that have just shed their hard shells. If they're harvested a little later they're called paper-thins—crabs with thin new shells. If you can't make it to Louisiana during buster or paper-thin season, then visit your local fish market to sample them.

 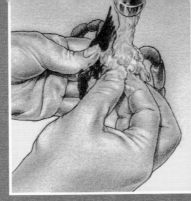 

4 Turn the crab over. Pull off the apron-shape piece and discard.

5 Thoroughly rinse crab under cold running water to remove the mustard-colored substance.

6 Pat the crab dry with paper towels. Now it's ready to fry!

Crawfish Boulettes

1 pound shelled crawfish tails *or* shrimp, cooked ¼ cup chopped green onions 2 cloves garlic, minced	● Devein crawfish or shrimp (see how-to, page 48). Chop into small pieces. Toss with green onions and garlic.
1 beaten egg ⅓ cup fine dry bread crumbs 2 tablespoons milk ½ teaspoon ground red pepper ¼ teaspoon salt	● Add egg, bread crumbs, milk, red pepper, and salt. Mix well. Shape mixture into balls, using about *1 tablespoon* mixture for each.
¼ cup fine dry bread crumbs Shortening *or* cooking oil for deep-fat frying	● Roll balls in bread crumbs. In a heavy saucepan or deep-fat fryer heat about 2 inches melted shortening or cooking oil to 375°. Fry balls in hot fat, a few at a time, for 30 to 60 seconds or just till golden. Remove and drain on paper towels. Keep warm in a 325° oven while frying remainder. Makes 4 to 6 servings.

Boulette means meatball in French, but these use crawfish or shrimp instead of meat. Serve these spicy morsels as a main course or an appetizer.

Early settlers hushed their barking dogs by tossing them these bready morsels. We bet a batch of hush puppies will quiet the growling stomachs at your house.

Hush Puppies

1 beaten egg ½ cup buttermilk *or* sour milk ¼ cup finely chopped green onions 1 tablespoon water	● In a small mixing bowl stir together egg, buttermilk or sour milk, green onions, and water.
¾ cup cornmeal ¼ cup all-purpose flour 2 tablespoons sugar 1 teaspoon baking powder ¼ teaspoon baking soda ⅛ teaspoon salt	● In a medium mixing bowl combine cornmeal, flour, sugar, baking powder, baking soda, and salt. Add egg mixture to dry ingredients. Stir just till moistened.
Shortening *or* cooking oil for deep-fat frying	● In a heavy saucepan or deep-fat fryer heat about 2 inches melted shortening or oil to 375°. Drop batter by tablespoons into hot fat. Fry a few at a time, about 2 minutes or till golden brown, turning once. Drain on paper towels. Keep warm in a 325° oven while frying remainder. Makes about 18.

Fried Frog Legs

2 pounds fresh *or* frozen frog legs	● Thaw frog legs, if frozen. Separate into individual legs.	Frog legs taste a lot like chicken. And, just like chicken pieces, frog legs vary in size. For 2 pounds, we used 14 legs (7 pairs) and cooked them for 1½ minutes. If you have fewer legs per pound, cook them a little longer.
⅓ cup milk ⅔ cup corn flour 1 teaspoon salt ½ teaspoon ground red pepper	● Dip frog legs in milk. In a small bowl combine corn flour, salt, and red pepper. Coat frog legs with corn flour mixture.	
Shortening *or* cooking oil for deep-fat frying Cocktail *or* Tartar Sauce (see recipes, page 49) Lemon halves Fresh herb (optional)	● In a saucepan or deep-fat fryer heat about 2 inches melted shortening or cooking oil to 375°. Fry coated frog legs, a few at a time, in deep hot fat for 1½ to 2 minutes or till done. Drain on paper towels. Keep warm in a 325° oven while frying remaining legs. Serve with Tartar Sauce or Cocktail Sauce and lemon. Garnish with a fresh herb, if desired. Makes 6 servings.	

Fry It!

Whether you're frying beignets or frog legs, the technique is the same. Here are a few tips.
● Use a deep-fat frying thermometer to measure the oil temperature accurately.
● Control the oil temperature by adjusting the heat and by frying only a few pieces at a time. Then, reheat the oil before adding more food.
● Use a slotted spoon to add and remove food.
● Drain just-fried food on paper towels or a wire rack.
● Save oil to reuse. Strain cooled oil through two layers of cheesecloth into jars. Cover and refrigerate.

**Fried Seafood Platter
(shrimp and oysters)**
(see recipe, page 48)

Cocktail Sauce
(see recipe, page 49)

Fried Frog Legs

Pan-Fried Catfish

1 pound fresh *or* frozen catfish fillets *or* other fish fillets	● Thaw fish, if frozen.	**Acadian waters abound with catfish. Cajuns lightly coat them with corn flour and fry them, transforming the sweet-tasting fresh-water fish into a gastronomic delight.**
¼ cup corn flour *or* all-purpose flour ½ teaspoon ground red pepper ¼ teaspoon ground black pepper ⅛ teaspoon salt	● In a dish combine corn or all-purpose flour, red pepper, black pepper, and salt. Dip fish fillets in flour mixture to coat.	
Shortening *or* cooking oil for shallow-fat frying Tartar Sauce (see recipe, page 49) (optional) Endive (optional) Lemon wedges (optional)	● In a 12-inch skillet heat ¼ inch melted shortening or cooking oil over medium heat till hot. 　Add fillets to the skillet in a single layer. Fry on 1 side about 3 minutes or till golden. Turn and fry 3 to 4 minutes more or till golden and fish flakes with a fork. Drain on paper towels. Serve with Tartar Sauce and garnish with endive and lemon, if desired. Serves 4.	**Since catfish fillets usually are about ¼ inch thick, we based our frying time on this thickness. If you choose a thicker fish fillet, fry it a little longer.**

Fried Seafood Platter

Pictured on pages 44-45.

2 **pounds fresh *or* frozen shrimp in shells, *or* 2 pints shucked oysters**	● Thaw shrimp, if frozen. Peel shrimp, leaving last section and tail intact. Devein and butterfly shrimp (see photos, right). Drain oysters. Pat shrimp or oysters dry with paper towels.
1 **beaten egg** 1 **cup all-purpose flour** 1 **cup cold water** 2 **tablespoons cooking oil** ½ **teaspoon sugar** ½ **teaspoon salt**	● For batter, in a medium bowl stir together egg, flour, water, cooking oil, sugar, and salt. Beat mixture with a rotary beater till smooth.
All-purpose flour	● Roll shrimp or oysters in flour to coat, then dip in batter.
Shortening *or* cooking oil for deep-fat frying **Cocktail Sauce *or* Tartar Sauce (see recipes, opposite)** **Lemon half (optional)**	● In a saucepan or deep-fat fryer heat about 2 inches melted shortening or cooking oil to 375°. Fry shrimp or oysters, a few at a time, for 2 to 3 minutes or till golden. Drain on paper towels. Keep warm in a 325° oven while frying remainder. Serve with Cocktail Sauce or Tartar Sauce and lemon, if desired. Makes 6 to 8 servings.

Any respectable fried seafood platter isn't complete without crispy Hush Puppies (see recipe, page 43).

To devein shrimp, peel the shell. Make a shallow slit along the back from head to tail. Use a knife tip to remove the black sand vein that runs along the back, as shown.

To butterfly shrimp, make a deeper slit along the back where you cut to devein. Cut only three-fourths of the way through. Lay the shrimp on a flat surface and open to resemble a butterfly.

Cocktail Sauce

Pictured on pages 44-45.

1 tablespoon finely chopped
   onion
1 clove garlic, minced
1 tablespoon butter *or*
   margarine

● In a 1-quart saucepan cook onion and garlic in butter or margarine till tender.

⅔ cup water
½ of a 6-ounce can (⅓ cup)
   tomato paste
1 tablespoon prepared
   horseradish
2 teaspoons lemon juice
½ teaspoon dry mustard
¼ teaspoon salt
¼ teaspoon ground red
   pepper
   Grated fresh horseradish
   (optional)

● Stir in the water, tomato paste, prepared horseradish, lemon juice, dry mustard, salt, and red pepper. Bring to boiling. Reduce heat. Simmer, uncovered, for 5 to 10 minutes or to desired consistency. Serve warm or chilled with fried fish and seafood. Top with grated fresh horseradish, if desired. Makes about ¾ cup sauce.

Serve flavor-packed Cocktail Sauce and creamy Tartar Sauce to complement Fried Frog Legs (see recipe, page 44), Pan-Fried Catfish (see recipe, page 46), or Fried Seafood Platter (see recipe, page 48).

Tartar Sauce

1 cup mayonnaise *or* salad
   dressing
¼ cup finely chopped sweet
   pickle
2 tablespoons finely
   chopped green onion
1 tablespoon snipped
   parsley
1 tablespoon lemon juice
   Dash bottled hot pepper
   sauce

● In a bowl stir together mayonnaise or salad dressing, sweet pickle, green onion, parsley, lemon juice, and hot pepper sauce. Serve with fried fish and seafood. Makes about 1¼ cups sauce.

Produce Pickin's

Sweet potato
(Louisiana yam)

Eggplant

Green (bell) pepper

Dried figs

Mirliton

Okra

Pecans

Can't tell mirlitons
from okra?
Here's a sampling
of Cajun crops that
will help you out.

Fry Coating

2 cups corn flour *or*
  all-purpose flour
2 teaspoons onion powder
  or garlic powder
2 teaspoons salt
1 teaspoon dried thyme,
  crushed
1 teaspoon ground black
  pepper

● In a mixing bowl combine corn flour or all-purpose flour, onion or garlic powder, salt, thyme, and black pepper. Use to coat fish, chicken, or vegetables. Store mix in tightly covered container in the refrigerator. Makes about 2 cups.

Pan-Fried Fish: In a shallow bowl combine 1 beaten *egg* and ½ cup *milk*. Dip 1 pound *fresh* or *thawed frozen fish fillets* in beaten egg mixture, then in ⅓ cup Fry Coating.

  In a 12-inch skillet heat ¼ inch melted *shortening* or *cooking oil*. Add fillets to skillet in a single layer. Fry on one side about 3 minutes or till golden. Turn and fry for 3 to 4 minutes more or till golden and fish flakes with a fork. Drain on paper towels. Makes 4 servings.

Fried Chicken: Rinse one 2½- to 3-pound *broiler-fryer chicken,* cut up. Pat dry with paper towels. In a shallow bowl combine 1 *egg* and ½ cup *milk*. In a plastic or paper bag place ⅓ cup Fry Coating. Dip chicken pieces in egg mixture. Then, add chicken, 2 or 3 pieces at a time, to the bag and shake to coat.

  In a 12-inch skillet heat 2 tablespoons melted *shortening* or *cooking oil*. Cook chicken, uncovered, over medium-low heat for 50 to 60 minutes or till tender, turning pieces occasionally. Remove chicken. Drain on paper towels. Serves 6.

Fried Vegetables: Dip 1 pound sliced and peeled *eggplant* or sliced *zucchini* or whole *mushrooms* in 1 beaten *egg*. Then, dip vegetables in ½ cup Fry Coating. Fry vegetables, a few at a time, in deep hot oil (375°) for 2 to 3 minutes or till crisp and golden. Drain on paper towels. Makes 4 servings.

Acadian grocery stores and large supermarkets in other areas stock commercial coating for Cajun fish fries. But just in case you can't get it in your area, here's our homemade version. Give chicken and vegetables as much gusto as fish with this zesty coating.

Cajun Cupboard

Peek into this cupboard. It's stocked with ingredients you may want to keep on hand when you're cooking Cajun. On the next few pages, you'll find homemade versions of the hard-to-get ones.

Crab Boil Seasoning

3 tablespoons mustard seed
3 tablespoons whole
   coriander
8 bay leaves, crumbled
1 tablespoon whole allspice
2 teaspoons whole cloves
1 teaspoon crushed red
   pepper

● In a double layer of cheesecloth combine mustard seed, whole coriander, bay leaves, whole allspice, cloves, and red pepper. Tie bag.

● To cook 4 pounds of seafood, place cheesecloth bag in 3 to 5 quarts boiling water with seafood. Makes 1 bag.

Put this seasoning to good use. Cook up some crawfish and crab for a Cajun-style get-together. Make two bags for the Crab Boil on page 38.

Three-Pepper Seasoning

2 tablespoons salt
1 tablespoon ground red
   pepper
1 teaspoon ground white
   pepper
1 teaspoon garlic powder
1 teaspoon ground black
   pepper

● In a tightly covered container combine salt, red pepper, white pepper, garlic powder, and black pepper. Store at room temperature. Use to season meats, fish, vegetables, and soups. Makes about ¼ cup seasoning.

Without a doubt, pepper ranks as the favorite seasoning in Acadia. Louisiana cooks often season foods with a mixture of ground black, white, and red peppers. The black pepper adds the aroma, the white pepper adds the bite, and the red pepper adds the burn.

CAUTION
DRIVER EATING BOUDIN

Boudin Blanc

7 to 8 feet pork casings

● Before making sausage mixture, run cool water through casings. Soak pork casings in water for 2 hours or overnight in the refrigerator.

3 cups water
1 pound lean boneless pork, cut into 1-inch cubes
8 ounces pork heart *or* kidneys, cut into 1-inch cubes
1 teaspoon salt
8 ounces pork liver, cut up

● In a Dutch oven combine water, pork, heart or kidneys, and salt. Bring to boiling. Reduce heat. Cover and simmer for 1 hour. Add liver. Cover and simmer about 10 minutes or till all meat is cooked. Drain and cool. With coarse blade of food grinder, grind together cooked meats and pork liver.

4 cups cold, cooked rice
2 large onions, finely chopped (2 cups)
1 green pepper, finely chopped (½ cup)
½ cup snipped parsley
½ cup thinly sliced green onion tops
2 teaspoons ground red pepper
1½ teaspoons salt

● Mix ground meats with rice, onions, green pepper, parsley, green onion tops, red pepper, and salt.

● Assemble sausage stuffer attachment to electric mixer or food grinder according to manufacturer's directions. (Don't use the cutting blade, or sausage will be twice-ground and mushy.) Using a 3- to 4-foot piece of casing at a time, slip one end and then the remaining length of the casing onto the medium or small stuffer tube.

● Force sausage mixture through tube till even with tube opening. Pull off 2 inches of casing and tie a knot. Fill casing firm but not overly full, twisting casing when links are 4 to 5 inches long. Wrap and chill sausages at once.

● Wrap in moisture- and vaporproof wrap. Store in the refrigerator for up to 4 days or freeze for up to 2 months before cooking.
  To serve, place links in an unheated skillet. Prick the casings. Add 3 cups cold *water*. Cover and cook over medium heat for 4 to 5 minutes or till heated through. Makes 3¼ pounds sausage (about 6 servings total).

Boudin (boo-DEN) is the fast food of Acadiana. So many Cajuns stop by convenience grocery stores to pick some up that you may even see a bumper sticker that reads:

CAUTION
Driver eating boudin.

Here's the official boudin eating guide: Bite into the sausage, but don't bite through. Pull the casing between your teeth so you eat just the filling.

After the pork casing fills with mixture, pull off 2 inches of casing and twist. The casing should be firm, but not overly full.

Sausage Sampler

Cajuns love spicy sausage. Over the years they have developed their own special varieties. Here are the favorites.

Homemade Boudin Blanc

Tasso

Andouille

Purchased Boudin

MILD

Maque Choux

8	**medium ears fresh corn**

● Remove corn from cob, cutting two-thirds of the way to the cob. Then, scrape the cob with the dull edge of a knife. You should have about 4 cups corn mixture. Set aside.

1	**medium onion, chopped (½ cup)**
½	**cup chopped green pepper**
2	**tablespoons butter *or* margarine**

● In a 3-quart saucepan over medium heat cook onion and green pepper in butter or margarine about 5 minutes or till vegetables are tender.

1	**medium tomato, cut up**
¼	**teaspoon salt**
¼	**teaspoon ground red pepper**
¼	**teaspoon ground black pepper**

● Stir in corn, tomato, salt, red pepper, and black pepper. Reduce heat to low. Cover and cook about 20 minutes or till corn is tender. Season to taste with salt. Makes 6 servings.

If you asked a Cajun to translate Maque Choux (MOCK shoo), he would tell you it means "smothered corn." In Louisiana, smothered means cooked with tomatoes, onion, and green pepper.

Smothered Okra

1 large onion, chopped
½ cup chopped green pepper
2 tablespoons butter *or* margarine

● In a 10-inch skillet cook onion and green pepper in butter or margarine about 5 minutes or till tender.

2 cups sliced okra *or* one 10-ounce package frozen cut okra, thawed
2 medium tomatoes, peeled, seeded, and chopped
¼ teaspoon salt
¼ teaspoon ground red pepper
⅛ teaspoon ground black pepper

● Stir in okra, tomatoes, salt, red pepper, and black pepper. Bring to boiling. Reduce heat. Cover and simmer for 30 to 35 minutes for fresh okra or about 15 minutes for frozen okra or till okra is tender. Makes 4 servings.

African slaves brought okra to Louisiana. Cajun cooks quickly adopted the green pod.

You'll find fresh okra in the supermarkets from June to September. Choose tender pods (either smooth or ridged) that range in color from light to deep green. Store okra in a plastic bag in your refrigerator for up to 2 weeks.

Baked Cheese Grits

2 cups water
½ cup instant grits
2 beaten eggs

● In a 1-quart saucepan bring water to boiling. Slowly stir in grits. Gradually stir about *1 cup* hot mixture into eggs. Return to saucepan. Remove from heat.

Serve this puffy, soufflé-like casserole with roast pork or duck for a down-home dinner.

1 cup shredded cheddar
    cheese (4 ounces)
¼ cup milk
¼ teaspoon ground white
    pepper

● Stir cheese, milk, and pepper into grits. Spoon into a 1-quart casserole. Bake in a 350° oven about 50 minutes or till puffed and a knife inserted in center comes out clean. Serves 4 to 6.

True Grits

Grits are to the South what potatoes are to the rest of the country. No meal is complete without them! Technically grits are coarsely ground corn kernels (sometimes called hominy grits). No matter what you call them, grits are great-tasting and easy to fix.

For breakfast, top hot cooked grits with butter and brown sugar to make a tasty hot cereal. Or, cook 'em with garlic and you've got the equivalent of hash browns to accompany ham and eggs.

For lunch or dinner, serve grits like cooked rice—smothered in a meat sauce or cooked red beans (see recipe, page 85). Or, bake 'em with cheese, as in the casserole recipe above.

Dirty Rice

1½ cups water ¾ cup long-grain rice	● In a small saucepan bring water and *uncooked* rice to boiling. Reduce heat. Cover and simmer about 20 minutes or till rice is done. Set rice aside.
4 ounces chicken livers 4 ounces chicken gizzards 4 ounces ground pork	● Cut chicken livers and gizzards into pieces. Use the coarse blade of a food grinder to grind livers and gizzards, *or* finely chop meat. Set aside. In a 2-quart saucepan cook pork over medium-high heat till meat loses its pink color. Add ground livers and gizzards. Cook till meat loses its pink color.
¾ cup chicken broth ½ cup chopped onion ⅓ cup chopped green pepper ¼ cup chopped celery 1 clove garlic, minced ½ teaspoon salt ¼ to ½ teaspoon ground red pepper ¼ to ½ teaspoon ground black pepper	● Stir in broth, onion, green pepper, celery, garlic, salt, red pepper, and black pepper. Bring to boiling. Reduce heat. Cover and simmer about 10 minutes or till gizzards are tender. Stir in rice and heat through. Makes 8 side-dish servings.

Don't let the name turn you off. Cajun humor often spills over into Cajun cooking. The "dirty" appearance comes from the chicken livers.

Roasted Piquant Pecans

¼ cup butter *or* margarine 2 tablespoons Worcestershire sauce 1 teaspoon bottled hot pepper sauce	● In a small saucepan melt butter or margarine. Stir in Worcestershire sauce and bottled hot pepper sauce.
1 pound pecan *or* walnut halves	● Spread pecan or walnut halves in a shallow baking pan. Drizzle with butter mixture. Toss to coat. Bake in a 350° oven for 15 to 20 minutes or till roasted, stirring occasionally. Makes 4 cups.

There must be jillions of recipes for Cajun country's tasty fresh commodity—pecans. Here's yet another: peppy nuts, coated with hot sauce, to eat as an out-of-the-hand snack.

1 Cook the mirlitons in boiling salted water until they're tender. Drain the squash and cool.

Stuffed Mirlitons

2 8-ounce mirliton squash	● Cook squash, covered, in enough boiling salted water to cover squash, about 40 minutes or till tender. Drain. When cool enough to handle, cut mirlitons lengthwise in half. Remove seeds. Scoop out pulp to within ½ inch of skin. Set shells aside. Chop pulp. Drain. Squeeze pulp between paper towels to remove excess liquid. Set aside.
1 **medium onion, chopped** ¼ **cup chopped celery** 1 **clove garlic, minced** ¼ **cup butter *or* margarine**	● For stuffing, cook onion, celery, and garlic in butter or margarine till tender. Remove from heat.
8 **ounces fresh *or* frozen cooked, shelled shrimp** 1 **cup soft bread crumbs, toasted (1¼ slices)** 2 **tablespoons snipped parsley** ⅛ **teaspoon salt** ⅛ **teaspoon ground red pepper** ⅛ **teaspoon ground black pepper** **Celery leaves (optional)**	● Reserve 4 whole shrimp for garnish, if desired. Cut remaining shrimp into small pieces. Stir shrimp, mirliton pulp, toasted bread crumbs, parsley, salt, red pepper, and black pepper into onion mixture. Spoon stuffing into squash shells. Place shells in a 10x6x2-inch baking dish. Bake stuffed squash, uncovered, in a 350° oven about 30 minutes or till heated through. Garnish each serving with celery leaves and a whole cooked shrimp, if desired. Makes 4 servings.

A mirliton (MILL-ee-tawn) is a pale green, tropical squash that grows in Acadia. In your area, you may find it going by its Latin American name, chayote (rhymes with coyote). No matter what its name, this squash has a crisp white flesh.

TOASTED BREAD CRUMBS

To toast bread crumbs, spread crumbs in a shallow baking pan. Bake in a 350° oven about 10 minutes or till toasted, stirring occasionally.

Stuffed Zucchini: Prepare as directed above, *except* substitute two 8-ounce zucchini for the mirlitons. Cook zucchini in water for 10 to 15 minutes. To bake, arrange shells in a 12x7½x2-inch baking dish. Continue as directed above, *except* bake 20 minutes.

2 Cut each squash in half lengthwise and remove the single flat seed.

3 Use a spoon to scoop out the pulp. Leave a ½-inch-thick shell.

Candied Yams

6 medium yams *or* sweet potatoes (2 pounds)	● Scrub yams or sweet potatoes and peel. Cut off woody portions and ends. Cut into 2-inch pieces.
¼ cup butter *or* margarine **1 cup orange juice** **½ cup sugar** **½ cup packed brown sugar** **¼ cup raisins** **¼ cup water** **2 thin slices orange** **2 thin slices lemon** **½ teaspoon ground cinnamon** **¼ teaspoon ground nutmeg**	● In a 4-quart Dutch oven melt butter or margarine over medium heat. Stir in orange juice, sugar, brown sugar, raisins, water, orange slices, lemon slices, cinnamon, and nutmeg. Add yams or sweet potatoes. Bring to boiling over high heat. Reduce heat to low. Cover and simmer for 15 to 20 minutes or till yams are just tender. Uncover and simmer about 15 minutes more or till yams are glazed, stirring occasionally. Makes 6 servings.

Cajuns are partial to their own home-grown sweet potatoes, called Louisiana yams, but you can use whatever type you find at your grocery store.

Praline Yam Casserole

6 medium yams *or* sweet potatoes (2 pounds)	● Scrub yams or sweet potatoes. Cut off woody portions and ends. In a 4-quart Dutch oven cook yams, covered, in enough boiling, salted water to cover for 25 to 30 minutes or till tender. Drain and cool slightly. Peel and cut up yams.
⅓ cup milk **¼ cup packed brown sugar** **¼ cup butter *or* margarine, melted** **1 egg** **1 teaspoon vanilla** **½ teaspoon salt**	● Mash yams with a potato masher or with an electric mixer on low speed. Add milk, brown sugar, butter or margarine, egg, vanilla, and salt. Beat till fluffy. Add additional milk, if desired. Turn into a greased 10x6x2-inch baking dish.
3 tablespoons butter *or* margarine **⅓ cup packed brown sugar** **3 tablespoons all-purpose flour** **⅓ cup chopped pecans**	● In a small saucepan melt butter or margarine over low heat. Stir in brown sugar, flour, and pecans. Mix well. Spoon pecan mixture over casserole. Bake in a 350° oven for 30 to 35 minutes or till heated through. Serves 8.

You can't go wrong with crunchy-sweet praline topping spooned over fluffy whipped yams. It's sure to star at your next gathering.

Eggplant Dressing

1 small eggplant	● Cut the top off the eggplant. Peel, if desired. Cut into ½-inch cubes. In a medium saucepan cook eggplant in a small amount of boiling, salted water about 5 minutes or till tender. Drain.

¼ pound bulk pork sausage
1 large onion, chopped
1 cup fine dry bread crumbs
1 beaten egg
⅓ to ½ cup milk
½ teaspoon salt
¼ teaspoon ground black
    pepper
	● In a large skillet cook sausage and onion over medium-high heat till sausage is brown. Remove from heat.
	    Stir in eggplant, bread crumbs, egg, milk, salt, and pepper. Turn into a greased 1-quart casserole. Bake in a 350° oven about 30 minutes or till dressing is heated through. Serves 8.

The Cajuns borrowed eggplant from their Italian neighbors in New Orleans. Once they found how well eggplant grew in their gardens, it became a Cajun cooking staple.

Look for eggplant that is firm and heavy for its size, with a dark, shiny, smooth skin and a fresh-looking green cap.

Rice, Rice, Rice!

What's a Cajun dish without rice? Unusual. So here's all the know-how for cooking this Cajun mainstay.

For starters: Plan on 1 cup of uncooked long-grain rice for six servings. Use twice as much water as rice. Then add some butter or margarine (about 1 tablespoon for *every* cup of uncooked rice) and some salt, if you want.

Here's how: In a saucepan combine the water, rice, butter or margarine, and salt. Cover with a tight-fitting lid. Bring to boiling. Reduce heat. Simmer for 15 minutes. Do not lift cover. Remove from heat. Let stand, covered, for 10 minutes. Then, fluff with a fork.

To serve: Use your imagination. Pile it in the center of the bowl or plate, scatter it around the edge, or serve it to the side.

Stuffed Peppers

6 large green peppers Salt	● Cut green peppers in half lengthwise. Remove seeds and membranes and discard. Cook the green pepper halves, uncovered, in boiling water for 5 minutes. Invert to drain. Sprinkle the insides of peppers lightly with salt.	**Like a fiddle and a banjo, ground pork and fresh oysters blend in harmony. The result is the delicious filling in these stuffed green peppers.**
½ pound ground pork 1 large onion, chopped ½ cup chopped celery 1 clove garlic, minced ½ pint shucked oysters, drained and chopped	● In a large saucepan cook pork, onion, celery, and garlic till pork is brown and onion is tender. Drain off fat. Stir in oysters. Cook oyster mixture, uncovered, about 2 minutes more.	
3 cups soft bread crumbs, toasted (4 slices bread) 1 large tomato, peeled, seeded, and chopped ½ teaspoon salt ¼ teaspoon ground black pepper	● Stir bread crumbs, tomato, salt, and pepper into pork mixture. Stuff peppers with bread crumb mixture.	
	● Place stuffed peppers in a 12x7½x2-inch baking dish. Bake, uncovered, in a 350° oven for 30 to 35 minutes or till hot. Makes 6 servings.	
	● **Note:** To toast bread crumbs, spread crumbs evenly in a shallow baking pan. Bake in a 350° oven about 10 minutes or till golden.	

Syrup Cake

1¾ cups all-purpose flour 2 teaspoons baking powder ½ teaspoon baking soda	● Grease and lightly flour a 9x9x2-inch baking pan. In a bowl stir together the flour, baking powder, and soda.
½ cup butter *or* margarine ⅓ cup sugar 1 egg ¼ cup cane syrup, *or* 2 tablespoons dark corn syrup *and* 2 tablespoons dark molasses	● In a mixer bowl beat the butter or margarine with an electric mixer on medium speed for 30 seconds. Add the sugar and beat till fluffy. Beat in the egg and cane syrup.
¾ cup milk Powdered sugar *or* desired frosting	● Add dry ingredients and milk alternately to beaten mixture, beating till combined. Spread batter in the prepared pan. Bake in a 350° oven about 25 minutes or till cake tests done. Cool in the pan on a wire rack. Sprinkle cooled cake with powdered sugar, or frost. Makes 9 servings.

Fields of Louisiana sugar cane yield a sweet Cajun favorite: cane syrup. If cane syrup isn't available in your area, substitute a mixture of dark corn syrup and dark molasses.

Fig Bars

¾ cup all-purpose flour ¼ teaspoon baking soda ¼ teaspoon ground cinnamon Dash salt ⅓ cup butter *or* margarine ⅓ cup packed brown sugar 1 egg ¾ cup Fig Filling (see recipe, page 68)	● Grease and lightly flour a 9x9x2-inch baking pan. In a bowl stir together flour, baking soda, cinnamon, and salt. In a mixer bowl beat butter or margarine with an electric mixer on medium speed for 30 seconds. Add brown sugar and beat till fluffy. Add egg and Fig Filling and beat well. Add flour mixture and beat till well mixed.
Powdered sugar	● Spread batter in the prepared pan. Bake in a 350° oven about 20 minutes or till done. Cool in pan on wire rack. Sift powdered sugar atop. Cut into bars. Makes 24 bars.

As soon as the pastry rises to the surface, press the center with a long-handled fork and twist it to look like a pig's ear.

Les Orielles de Cochon

2 cups all-purpose flour **½ teaspoon salt**	● In a bowl stir together flour and salt. Set aside.
2 eggs **¼ cup butter *or* margarine, melted and cooled** **2 tablespoons water**	● In a deep bowl beat eggs with a fork or wire whisk. Gradually beat in the cooled butter or margarine. Stir in water. Stir into flour mixture till well combined. If necessary, use hands to work in flour. Form into a ball with hands. Divide dough into 24 balls. On a lightly floured surface roll each ball into a paper-thin round, 6 inches in diameter. Cover rounds to prevent drying.
Shortening *or* cooking oil for deep-fat frying	● In a large deep saucepan or deep-fat fryer heat 2 inches of melted shortening or cooking oil to 375°. Place one round of dough in the oil. As soon as it rises to the surface, press the center with a long-handled fork and twist the fork to give the dough a pig's ear shape. Press fork and dough against side of the pan to retain shape. Fry for ½ to 1 minute or till golden, turning once. Drain on paper towels. Repeat with remaining rounds.
1½ cups cane syrup *or* 1 cup dark corn syrup *plus* ½ cup light molasses **¾ cup coarsely chopped pecans**	● In a 2-quart saucepan bring cane syrup or syrup-molasses mixture to boiling. Clip a candy thermometer to pan. Cook syrup over medium-low heat to 230°, stirring frequently. Arrange the pastries on a platter. Drizzle with hot syrup. Sprinkle with pecans. Makes 24.

Les Orielles de Cochon (lay zaw-RE-y day kaw-SHOHN) is French for pig's ears. Why the funny name? Because as you fry these sweet treats, you twist them to look like a pig's ears.

Sweet Dough Pies

2 cups all-purpose flour 1½ teaspoons baking powder ¼ teaspoon salt	● In a small mixing bowl stir together flour, baking powder, and salt.
1 egg ¼ cup water 3 tablespoons sugar ¼ cup butter *or* margarine, melted and cooled	● In a medium mixing bowl beat together egg, water, and sugar. Stir in butter or margarine. Stir in dry ingredients till mixture forms a ball. Turn out onto a lightly floured surface. Knead 10 times. Divide dough into 8 portions.
Fig Filling (see recipe, below) *or* one 21-ounce can lemon pie filling	● Roll each portion to form a ¼-inch-thick circle, about 6 inches in diameter. Spoon a generous *3 tablespoons* filling in the center of each circle. Moisten edges. Fold circle in half. Seal edges with the tines of a fork. Bake in a 350° oven for 20 to 25 minutes or till golden. Cool on a wire rack. Makes 8.

Fig Filling: In a medium saucepan combine 1 cup snipped *dried figs* and 1 cup *water*. Bring to boiling. Reduce heat. Cover and simmer 20 minutes. Remove from heat. Stir in ⅓ cup *light corn syrup*. Mix ⅓ cup *sugar,* ¼ cup all-purpose *flour,* and dash *salt*. Stir into fig mixture. Cook and stir till thickened and bubbly. Remove from heat. Stir in 1 tablespoon *lemon juice*. Cool. Makes 1¾ cups.

Many Cajuns have never made a sweet dough pie in their lives—they get them at their local bakeries. But non-Cajuns don't have that luxury. We've included this recipe so non-Cajuns and Cajuns alike can enjoy making the turnovers at home.

Jumbo Pralines

Appease your sweet tooth with pralines (PRAW-leens). They're a Southern favorite that will put you in candy ecstasy. For petite pralines, spoon the mixture by tablespoons onto the lined baking sheets to form twenty-four 2-inch pralines.

1½ cups sugar
1½ cups packed brown sugar
 1 cup light cream

● Butter the sides of a heavy 2-quart saucepan. In the saucepan combine sugar, brown sugar, and cream. Cook over medium-high heat to boiling, stirring constantly with a wooden spoon to dissolve sugars. This should take 6 to 8 minutes. Avoid splashing the mixture on sides of the pan.

● Carefully clip a candy thermometer to pan. Cook over medium-low heat, stirring occasionally, till thermometer registers 234°, soft-ball stage. Mixture should boil at a moderate, steady rate over entire surface. Reaching soft-ball stage should take 18 to 20 minutes.

3 tablespoons butter *or* margarine
2 cups pecan halves (8 ounces)

● Remove pan from heat. Add butter or margarine but *do not stir.* Cool, without stirring, to 150° (about 30 minutes). Remove thermometer. Immediately stir in pecans. Beat vigorously with a wooden spoon till candy is just beginning to thicken but is still glossy. This should take 2 to 3 minutes.

● Drop about 2 tablespoons candy from a large serving spoon onto baking sheets lined with waxed paper, forming 3-inch pralines. If candy becomes too stiff to drop, stir in a few drops of *hot water.* Store in a tightly covered container. Makes 15 large pralines.

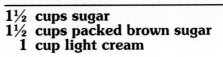

Bread Pudding With Whiskey Sauce

½ loaf French bread
2 cups milk
½ cup chopped pitted dates
   or raisins

● Tear bread into small pieces. (You should have 4 cups.) Combine bread, milk, and dates. Let stand 15 minutes or till bread is softened, stirring often.

Use up leftover French bread in this elegant fruit-filled pudding.

3 slightly beaten eggs
1 cup sugar
¼ cup butter *or* margarine, melted
1 tablespoon vanilla
2 teaspoons ground cinnamon
   Whiskey Sauce (see recipe, below)

● Beat together eggs, sugar, melted butter, vanilla, and cinnamon. Stir into bread mixture till blended. Turn into a greased 8x8x2-inch baking dish.

Bake in a 350° oven for 40 to 50 minutes or till a knife inserted in center comes out clean. Serve warm with Whiskey Sauce. Garnish with apple chunks and sweet woodruff or mint leaves, if desired. Makes 9 servings.

Whiskey Sauce: In a small saucepan melt ¼ cup *butter* or *margarine*. Stir in ½ cup *sugar*, 1 *egg yolk*, and 2 tablespoons *water*. Cook and stir over medium-low heat for 5 to 6 minutes or till sugar dissolves and mixture thickens. Remove from heat and stir in 2 tablespoons *bourbon*. Makes ⅔ cup.

Fruit Bread Pudding with Meringue Topping

3½ cups toasted white bread cubes (about 5 slices)
1 8¼-ounce can crushed pineapple, drained, *or* one 16-ounce can peaches *or* pears, drained and chopped (1⅓ cups)
½ cup raisins *or* chopped pecans

● In a greased 8x8x2-inch baking dish arrange *half* of the bread cubes. Spoon fruit and raisins or pecans over bread. Top with remaining bread cubes.

Cajuns mix up as many kinds of bread pudding as there are ingredients to put in desserts. In this version, you mix fruit with the bread cubes and top it off with a meringue.

4 slightly beaten egg yolks
2 cups milk
½ cup sugar
3 tablespoons butter *or* margarine, melted
1½ teaspoons vanilla
¼ teaspoon almond extract
⅛ teaspoon salt

● In a large mixing bowl beat together egg yolks, milk, sugar, butter or margarine, vanilla, almond extract, and salt. Pour over fruit and bread.
Bake in a 350° oven for 35 to 40 minutes or till a knife inserted in the center comes out clean. Remove from oven. Increase oven temperature to 450°.

4 egg whites
¼ teaspoon cream of tartar
½ cup sugar

● For meringue, in a large mixer bowl beat egg whites and cream of tartar with an electric mixer on high speed till soft peaks form (tips curl). Gradually add sugar, 1 tablespoon at a time, beating till stiff peaks form (tips stand straight).

● Gently spread the meringue evenly over the hot baked pudding. Return dish to oven and bake in a 450° oven for 4 to 5 minutes more or till meringue is golden. Serve warm. Makes 9 servings.

Sweet Potato-Molasses Pie

3 medium sweet potatoes *or* **yams (1½ pounds)** *or* **one 17-ounce can sweet potatoes**	● In a medium saucepan cook raw sweet potatoes in enough boiling salted water to cover for 20 to 25 minutes or till tender. Drain. Cool slightly and peel. Mash cooled or canned sweet potatoes. (You should have 1½ cups.) Set aside.	**Sweet potato pie looks and tastes like pumpkin pie. We dressed up our version with molasses to give it a hint of gingerbread flavor.**
Pastry for Single-Crust Pie (see recipe, page 39)	● Prepare Pastry for Single-Crust Pie. Line a 9-inch pie plate with the pastry. Trim and flute edge. Set aside the pie shell while preparing the filling.	
½ cup packed brown sugar **½ cup molasses** **1 teaspoon ground cinnamon** **½ teaspoon ground ginger** **½ teaspoon ground nutmeg** **¼ teaspoon salt** **3 slightly beaten eggs** **1 cup milk**	● In a large mixing bowl combine mashed sweet potatoes, brown sugar, molasses, cinnamon, ginger, nutmeg, and salt. Add eggs and milk to the sweet potato mixture. Mix well.	
	● Place pastry-lined pie plate in a 375° oven. Pour in sweet potato mixture. Cover edge of pie with foil. Bake in a 375° oven for 20 minutes. Remove the foil. Bake for 30 to 35 minutes more or till a knife inserted halfway between the center and edge comes out clean.	
Sweetened whipped cream (optional)	● Cool on a wire rack. Cover and chill to store. Serve with sweetened whipped cream, if desired. Makes 8 servings.	

Fais-Do-Do

Let's have a fais-do-do (fay-doe-DOE)! This Cajun party offers lots of fun, dancing, and good food. While twilight falls, the adults celebrate as the children nod off to sleep. That's why it's called fais-do-do (Cajun baby talk meaning make-sleep-sleep).

We've got the ideas for the good food. All you need are the people and the music. (See recipes, pages 76–79.)

Spiced Fig Cake

French Bread

Party Relish Tray

Shrimp and Ham
Jambalaya

Fais-Do-Do

THE MENU

Shrimp and Ham
Jambalaya

Party Relish Tray

French Bread
(See recipe, page 78)

Spiced Fig Cake
(See recipe, page 79)

Lemonade

MAKING IT HAPPEN

Several Hours Ahead:
● Make French Bread.
● Make Spiced Fig Cake.
● Make lemonade. Chill.
● Organize serving platters, plates, and utensils.

1½ Hours Ahead:
● Cut up and marinate the vegetables for Party Relish Tray.
● Cook Shrimp and Ham Jambalaya.

At Serving Time:
● Arrange marinated vegetables and greens on a serving tray.
● Sprinkle the cake with powdered sugar.
● Get the fiddlers pickin' and HAVE FUN!!!

Party Relish Tray

Pictured on pages 74-75.

⅓ cup vinegar
¼ cup salad oil
2 tablespoons lemon juice
2 teaspoons sugar
8 ounces whole mushrooms
2 cups cauliflower flowerets
3 medium carrots, cut into sticks

● For marinade, in a medium mixing bowl combine vinegar, salad oil, lemon juice, and sugar.
  Add mushrooms, cauliflower, and carrots. Toss to coat. Place in a plastic bag in a bowl. Seal tightly.
  Let stand for 1 hour at room temperature or several hours in the refrigerator, turning occasionally to distribute marinade evenly.

Although not officially Cajun, this marinated salad complements jambalaya perfectly!

Assorted greens

● Using a slotted spoon, remove vegetables from marinade. On a large serving platter arrange marinated vegetables on greens. Drizzle some of the remaining marinade over vegetables. Makes 6 servings.

Shrimp and Ham Jambalaya

Pictured on pages 74-75.

1 cup long-grain rice	● Cook rice according to package directions. Set aside.

4 cups water
½ cup purchased *or* homemade crab boil seasoning (**see recipe, page 53**)
1 pound fresh *or* frozen shrimp in shells
	● In a large saucepan combine water and crab boil seasoning. Bring to boiling. Reduce heat. Cover and simmer mixture for 15 minutes.
	    Add the fresh or frozen shrimp in shells. Return to boiling. Reduce heat and simmer about 3 minutes or till shrimp turn pink.
	    Drain. Peel shrimp under running water. Remove vein that runs down the back (see photo, page 48). Set aside.

1 cup chopped celery 1 medium onion, chopped (½ cup) 1 clove garlic, minced 2 tablespoons butter *or* margarine	● In a 3-quart saucepan cook celery, onion, and garlic in butter or margarine till vegetables are tender.
1 16-ounce can tomatoes, cut up 1 6-ounce can tomato paste ⅓ cup water 1 teaspoon Worcestershire sauce	● Stir in the *undrained* tomatoes, tomato paste, water, and Worcestershire sauce. Bring to boiling. Reduce heat. Cover and simmer 15 minutes.
2 cups cubed fully cooked ham Bottled hot pepper sauce	● Stir cooked rice, shrimp, and ham into tomato mixture. Season to taste with hot pepper sauce. Cook, uncovered, till mixture is heated through, stirring occasionally. Makes 6 servings.

Simmering the crab boil awhile before adding the shrimp ensures that the cooked shrimp will have plenty of flavor.

French Bread

Pictured on pages 74-75.

5½ to 6 cups all-purpose flour
2 packages active dry yeast
2 teaspoons salt
2 cups warm water
   (115° to 120°)

● In large mixer bowl combine *2 cups* of flour, yeast, and salt. Add warm water. Beat with an electric mixer on low speed for ½ minute, scraping sides of bowl constantly. Beat 3 minutes on high speed. Using a spoon, stir in as much of the remaining flour as you can.

There's hardly a Cajun meal that doesn't include French bread. It goes with everything.

In some Cajun bakeries rosy lights wink to signal when the fresh bread is ready, hot from the oven.

● Turn out onto a lightly floured surface. Knead in enough of the remaining flour to make a stiff dough that is smooth and elastic (8 to 10 minutes total). Shape into a ball. Place in a lightly greased bowl. Turn once to grease surface. Cover and let rise in warm place till double (1 to 1¼ hours) or let rise overnight in the refrigerator.

Cornmeal
1 slightly beaten egg white
   (optional)
1 tablespoon water
   (optional)

● Punch down. Turn out onto lightly floured surface. Divide in half. Cover and let rest 10 minutes. Roll each half into a 15x12-inch rectangle. Roll up tightly from long side. Seal well. Taper ends. (Or, shape into individual loaves or hard rolls as directed below.) Place, seam side down, on a greased baking sheet sprinkled with cornmeal. If desired, brush with mixture of egg white and water.

● Cover and let rise till nearly double (about 45 minutes). With a sharp knife, make 3 or 4 diagonal cuts about ¼ inch deep across tops of loaves.
   Bake in a 375° oven for 40 to 45 minutes. If desired, brush again with egg white mixture after 20 minutes of baking. Cool on wire rack. Makes 2 loaves.

Individual Loaves: Cut each half of dough into quarters, making 8 pieces total. Shape into balls. Cover and let rest 10 minutes. Shape each ball into a 6-inch loaf and taper ends. Place 2½ inches apart on a greased baking sheet sprinkled with cornmeal. Press down ends of loaves. Brush with egg white mixture, if desired. Cover and let rise till nearly double (about 45 minutes). Make 3 shallow cuts diagonally across top of each. Bake in a 375° oven for 25 to 30 minutes. If desired, brush again with egg white mixture after 15 minutes of baking. Makes 8 loaves.

Hard Rolls: Cut each half of dough into eighths, making 16 pieces total. Cover and let rest 10 minutes. Shape into rolls and place 2 inches apart on a greased baking sheet sprinkled with cornmeal. Brush with egg white mixture, if desired. Cover and let rise till nearly double (about 45 minutes). Cut a shallow crisscross in tops. Bake in a 375° oven 25 to 30 minutes. If desired, brush again with egg white mixture after baking 15 minutes. Makes 16.

Spiced Fig Cake

Pictured on pages 74-75.

3 cups all-purpose flour 2 teaspoons baking powder ½ teaspoon baking soda ½ teaspoon ground cinnamon ¼ teaspoon ground cloves	● Grease and lightly flour a 10-inch fluted tube pan. Set aside. In a bowl stir together flour, baking powder, baking soda, cinnamon, and cloves.
1 cup butter *or* margarine 1 cup sugar 1 teaspoon vanilla 4 eggs	● In a large mixer bowl beat butter or margarine with an electric mixer on medium speed for 30 seconds. Add sugar and vanilla. Beat till fluffy. Add eggs, one at a time, beating on medium speed 1 minute after each.
1 cup Fig Filling (see recipe, page 68) ¾ cup buttermilk *or* sour milk	● In a small bowl stir together Fig Filling and buttermilk or sour milk. Add dry ingredients and fig mixture alternately to beaten mixture, beating on low speed after each addition just till mixture is combined.
Powdered sugar	● Spoon batter into prepared pan. Bake in a 350° oven for 45 to 50 minutes or till cake tests done. Place cake on a wire rack. Cool 10 minutes. Remove from pan. Cool on rack. Sprinkle with powdered sugar. Makes 12 servings.

Figs grow in most climates. But the humidity in Louisiana causes them to spoil quickly once they're ripe. Fig desserts are just one way to use up the delicious surplus.

King's Cake

3½ to 4 cups all-purpose flour
1 package active dry yeast
½ cup milk
⅓ cup sugar
¼ cup butter *or* margarine
½ teaspoon salt

● In a large mixer bowl combine *1½ cups* of the flour and yeast. In a saucepan heat milk, sugar, butter or margarine, and salt till warm (115° to 120°) and butter or margarine is almost melted, stirring constantly.

Decorated in traditional Mardi Gras colors of green and yellow, King's Cake is first served on January 6, the Twelfth Night. Whoever gets the hidden pecan in his or her piece becomes the king or queen for the week and bakes another King's Cake. This festive ritual continues each week until Mardi Gras, the day before Lent.

3 eggs
½ cup diced candied citron

● Add heated mixture to flour mixture. Add eggs. Beat with an electric mixer on low speed for ½ minute, scraping bowl. Beat 3 minutes on high speed. Stir in citron. Using a spoon, stir in as much of the remaining flour as you can.

● Turn out onto a lightly floured surface. Knead in enough of the remaining flour to make a moderately stiff dough that is smooth and elastic (6 to 8 minutes total).
  Shape into a ball. Place in a greased bowl. Turn once to grease surface. Cover. Let rise in a warm place till double (1½ to 2 hours). Punch dough down. Cover. Let rest 10 minutes.

1 pecan half

● Press the pecan into the dough. Shape dough into a 30-inch-long roll. Join ends to form a ring about 10 inches in diameter. Place on a greased baking sheet. Cover and let rise till almost double (about 1 hour).
  Bake in a 350° oven for 25 to 30 minutes or till golden. If necessary, cover loosely with foil after 20 minutes to prevent overbrowning. Cool on a rack.

1 cup sifted powdered sugar
½ teaspoon vanilla
  Milk
  Green- *and* yellow-colored sugar

● In a small bowl beat together powdered sugar, vanilla, and enough milk (1 to 2 tablespoons) to make a thin frosting. Spoon the frosting over cooled cake. Sprinkle the colored sugar in 2-inch rows, spoke fashion, alternating colors around the top of the cake. Makes 12 to 16 servings.

Oysters Bienville

24	oysters in shells Coarse rock salt	● Open oysters in shells (see photo, right). With a knife, remove oysters from shells and drain well. Wash shells. Place each oyster in the deep half of each shell. Arrange on a bed of coarse rock salt in shallow pans. (*Or,* steady shells on pan lined with crumpled foil.)
½ 1 3	cup finely chopped green onions clove garlic, minced tablespoons butter *or* margarine	● In a saucepan cook green onions and garlic in butter or margarine about 5 minutes or till tender.
⅓ ¼ ¼ ¼ 1 ½ 3	cup all-purpose flour teaspoon salt teaspoon ground white pepper teaspoon ground red pepper cup chicken broth cup whipping cream beaten egg yolks	● Stir in flour, salt, white pepper, and red pepper. Add chicken broth and cream, stirring till well blended. Cook and stir over medium heat till the mixture is thickened and bubbly. Reduce heat. Gradually stir about *half* of mixture into beaten yolks. Return egg mixture to saucepan. Bring to a gentle boil. Cook and stir 2 minutes more.
½ ½ 2	pound cooked, shelled shrimp, chopped cup finely chopped fresh mushrooms tablespoons dry white wine	● Stir in shrimp, mushrooms, and wine. Heat through. Remove from heat. Spoon *2 tablespoons* of the shrimp mixture over each oyster.
¼ 2 ⅛	cup grated Parmesan cheese tablespoons fine dry bread crumbs teaspoon paprika	● Combine Parmesan cheese, bread crumbs, and paprika. Sprinkle over oysters. Bake in a 400° oven for 15 to 20 minutes or till golden on top and oysters curl. Makes 4 servings.

For lots of extra flavor in Oysters Bienville, cook the shrimp in crab-boil-seasoned water. You'll find a recipe for homemade Crab Boil Seasoning on page 53.

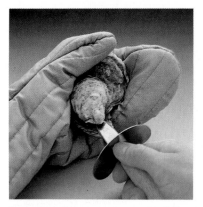

To shuck an oyster, hold the oyster in an oven mitt with the flat side up. Using a strong-bladed oyster knife, insert the knife tip into the hinge between the shells, as shown. Twist the blade to pry open the oyster. Slip the blade along the inside of the upper shell to free the muscle from the shell. Remove and discard the flat top shell. Slide the knife under the oyster to cut the muscle from the bottom shell. Reserve the deep bottom shells for Oysters Bienville.

Shrimp Rémoulade

3 cups water
1 lemon, cut into quarters
2 bay leaves
2 garlic cloves, cut in half
1½ teaspoons salt
½ teaspoon ground red pepper

● In a saucepan combine water, lemon, bay leaves, garlic, salt, and red pepper. Bring to boiling. Reduce heat. Simmer, uncovered, 10 minutes.

Serve *Shrimp Rémoulade* (RAY-moo-laud) as a cool entrée or as a make-ahead appetizer.

---

1 pound fresh *or* frozen peeled and deveined shrimp

● Turn heat to high. Add shrimp. Simmer for 1 to 3 minutes or till shrimp turn pink. Drain off liquid and discard lemon and bay leaves. Cool shrimp.

---

2 tablespoons vinegar
2 tablespoons prepared Creole-style *or* German-style mustard
2 teaspoons prepared horseradish
1½ teaspoons paprika
¼ teaspoon salt
⅛ teaspoon ground black pepper
Dash bottled hot pepper sauce
2 tablespoons olive *or* salad oil
¼ cup sliced green onions
2 tablespoons snipped parsley

● In a small mixer bowl combine vinegar, mustard, horseradish, paprika, salt, pepper, and hot pepper sauce. Slowly add olive or salad oil, beating well with an electric mixer. Stir in green onions and snipped parsley.
   In a medium mixing bowl stir together cooked shrimp and oil mixture. Cover and chill for 4 to 24 hours, stirring shrimp occasionally.

Lettuce leaves

● Using a slotted spoon, spoon shrimp mixture atop lettuce on a platter. Makes 4 main-dish servings.

Red Beans and Rice

1 pound dry red beans *or* dry red kidney beans **6 cups cold water**	● Rinse beans. In a large Dutch oven cover beans with cold water. Bring to boiling. Reduce heat. Simmer for 2 minutes. Remove from heat. Cover and let stand for 1 hour. (Or, in a covered pan soak beans in water overnight in a cool place.) Drain and rinse beans.
6 cups hot water **1 pound meaty ham bone *or* smoked pork hocks** **1 large onion, chopped (1 cup)** **3 cloves garlic, minced** **2 bay leaves** **½ to ¾ teaspoon ground red pepper**	● In the same Dutch oven combine rinsed beans, hot water, ham bone or pork hocks, onion, garlic, bay leaves, and red pepper. Bring to boiling. Reduce heat. Cover and simmer about 2½ hours or till beans are tender, adding more water, if necessary, and stirring the bean mixture occasionally.
1 pound smoked sausage, cut into bite-size pieces	● Remove ham bone or hocks. When ham bone is cool enough to handle, cut meat from bone. Discard bone. Chop meat. Return meat to pan. Stir in sausage. Cook gently, uncovered, for 20 to 30 minutes more or till a thick gravy forms, stirring mixture occasionally.
Hot cooked rice **Sliced green onions**	● Remove bay leaves. Serve red bean mixture over hot cooked rice. Sprinkle with green onions. Makes 8 servings.
	● **Note:** Freeze any leftover bean mixture in 2- or 4-cup portions in freezer containers. To serve, place frozen mixture in saucepan. Cover and cook over medium-low heat till heated through, breaking mixture apart and stirring occasionally. (Cook about 30 minutes for 2 cups mixture. Cook 45 minutes for 4 cups mixture.) Add water for desired consistency. The mixture should be the consistency of thick chili.

In the old days, *Red Beans and Rice* was the wash-day supper. Early Monday morning, the washing began and the beans were put on to cook. By the end of the day, the clean laundry was folded and the beans were ready to eat. Our version trims hours from the original cooking time. But the flavor is still as full and rich.

Bananas Foster

4 ripe small bananas **Lemon juice**	● Peel bananas and cut in half lengthwise, then crosswise. Brush bananas with some lemon juice to prevent darkening.
⅔ cup packed brown sugar **⅓ cup butter _or_ margarine**	● In a skillet or blazer pan of a chafing dish, heat brown sugar and butter or margarine over medium heat till mixture melts, stirring occasionally.
Dash ground cinnamon **2 tablespoons banana liqueur**	● Add bananas to the sugar mixture and cook, uncovered, for 3 to 4 minutes, turning once. Sprinkle with cinnamon. Drizzle banana liqueur atop.
3 tablespoons rum **Vanilla ice cream**	● In a small saucepan heat the rum just till warm. Ignite and pour the rum over the banana mixture. Serve over vanilla ice cream. Makes 4 servings.

Just close your eyes—then bite into a spoonful of Bananas Foster. This dessert tastes so rich that you can almost imagine yourself sitting in an elegant New Orleans restaurant.

Shrimp Creole

1 pound fresh *or* frozen peeled and deveined shrimp 1 medium onion, chopped (½ cup) ½ cup chopped green pepper ½ cup chopped celery 2 cloves garlic, minced ¼ cup butter *or* margarine	● Thaw shrimp, if frozen. In a 10-inch skillet cook onion, green pepper, celery, and garlic in butter or margarine till tender but not brown.
1 16-ounce can tomatoes, cut up 2 tablespoons snipped parsley ½ teaspoon salt ½ teaspoon paprika ¼ to ½ teaspoon ground red pepper 1 bay leaf	● Add *undrained* tomatoes, parsley, salt, paprika, red pepper, and bay leaf. Bring to boiling. Reduce heat. Cover and simmer 15 minutes.
2 tablespoons cold water 4 teaspoons cornstarch Hot cooked rice Parsley sprigs (optional)	● Combine cold water and cornstarch. Stir into tomato mixture. Stir in shrimp. Cook and stir till thickened and bubbly, then cook and stir 2 minutes more. Remove bay leaf. Serve over rice. Garnish with parsley, if desired. Serves 4.

Shrimp ranks as the most popular seafood around. It's sold by size or count per pound. Use medium shrimp (about 24 per pound) in *Shrimp Creole.*

Po' Boys

1 pint shucked oysters 2 eggs ¾ cup corn flour *or* all-purpose flour ½ teaspoon salt ¼ teaspoon ground black pepper	● Drain oysters. Pat dry with paper towels. In a small mixing bowl beat eggs. In another mixing bowl combine flour, salt, and pepper. Dip oysters into beaten eggs, then coat with flour mixture.
Shortening *or* cooking oil for deep-fat frying	● In a saucepan or deep-fat fryer heat 2 inches shortening or oil to 375°. Fry oysters, a few at a time, in hot oil for 1 to 1½ minutes or till golden. Drain on paper towels. Keep warm in a 325° oven while frying remaining oysters.
2 7-inch-long loaves French bread, sliced horizontally 2 tablespoons butter *or* margarine, softened 2 tablespoons mayonnaise *or* salad dressing Bottled hot pepper sauce Lemon wedges	● Spread the cut side of each loaf bottom with butter or margarine. Heat in a 325° oven about 5 minutes till warm. Spread the cut side of each loaf top with mayonnaise or salad dressing. Heap fried oysters onto bottoms of the loaves. Sprinkle oysters with hot pepper sauce. Add loaf tops. Serve sandwiches warm with lemon wedges. Makes 2 servings.

Long ago, tardy Cajun husbands knew the value of fried oysters. They offered this take-out sandwich as a peacemaker to angry waiting wives.

Turtle Soup

1 pound boneless turtle, cut into 1-inch cubes ¼ cup cooking oil ¼ cup all-purpose flour	● In a 4-quart Dutch oven or saucepan cook turtle meat in hot oil over medium-high heat till brown. Remove turtle meat. Stir in flour. Cook over medium-high heat 4 to 5 minutes, stirring constantly, or till a reddish-brown roux forms. (See pages 6-7.)
½ cup chopped onion ½ cup chopped celery ½ cup chopped green pepper 2 cloves garlic, minced	● Add chopped onion, celery, green pepper, and garlic. Cook about 10 minutes or till vegetables are tender.
1 16-ounce can tomatoes, cut up 2 cups beef broth ½ teaspoon salt ⅛ teaspoon dried thyme, crushed ⅛ teaspoon ground allspice ⅛ teaspoon ground black pepper 1 bay leaf	● Add turtle meat, *undrained* tomatoes, broth, salt, thyme, allspice, pepper, and bay leaf. Bring to boiling. Reduce heat. Cover and simmer mixture about 40 minutes or till meat is tender.
¼ cup dry sherry 2 hard-cooked eggs, chopped Lemon slices	● Stir in sherry. Cover and cook 10 minutes more. Remove bay leaf. Garnish with eggs and lemon. Makes 4 servings.

One pound boneless turtle equals about 1⅓ pounds turtle meat with the bone. Ask for turtle at your local fish market.

Can't find turtle? Substitute pork cut into ¾-inch cubes.

Doberge Cake

Lemon Filling (see recipe, below)
2¼ cups all-purpose flour
2 teaspoons baking powder
¼ teaspoon salt

● Prepare and cool the Lemon Filling. Grease and lightly flour three 8x1½-inch round baking pans. Set aside. In a medium mixing bowl combine flour, baking powder, and salt.

Ingenious New Orleans bakers took the famous European dobos torte and fashioned the New Orleans facsimile—Doberge (DO-bash) Cake.

Our version meets the minimum height requirement—it's six layers tall. If you have only two cake pans, bake two layers at a time.

½ cup butter *or* margarine
¼ cup shortening
1½ cups sugar
1 teaspoon vanilla
3 egg yolks

● In a large mixer bowl beat butter or margarine and shortening with an electric mixer on medium speed for 30 seconds. Gradually add sugar and vanilla, beating till light and fluffy. Add egg yolks, one at a time, beating 1 minute after each.

¾ cup milk
3 stiff-beaten egg whites

● Add dry ingredients and milk alternately to beaten mixture, beating after each addition till blended. Gently fold in egg whites by hand.

LEMON ICING
In a mixer bowl beat two softened 3-ounce packages *cream cheese,* and 3 cups sifted *powdered sugar* till fluffy. Add 1 teaspoon finely shredded *lemon peel* and ¼ teaspoon *vanilla* and beat till smooth.

● To make the 6 cake layers, transfer a generous ¾ *cup* of batter into each prepared pan, spreading evenly over the bottom of pan. Bake in a 375° oven for 10 to 12 minutes or till cakes test done. Cool 5 minutes in pans. Remove from pans and cool on wire racks.
Wash, grease, and flour pans. Spoon the remaining batter into the 3 pans. Bake and cool as directed above.

Lemon Icing
(see recipe, right)
Shredded lemon peel
(optional)

● To assemble, place 1 cake layer on serving plate. Spread a scant ½ *cup* Lemon Filling evenly atop. Repeat with 4 more layers and filling. Top with final layer. Cover and chill thoroughly. Spread Lemon Icing over top and sides of cake. Cover and store in the refrigerator. Before serving, sprinkle top with shredded lemon peel, if desired. Makes 16 servings.

Lemon Filling: In a saucepan combine 1¼ cups *sugar,* 3 tablespoons *cornstarch,* 3 tablespoons *all-purpose flour,* and dash *salt.* Stir in 1½ cups *cold water.* Cook and stir till thickened and bubbly. Cook and stir 2 minutes more.
Stir about *1 cup* of the hot mixture into 3 beaten *egg yolks.* Return mixture to saucepan. Bring mixture to a gentle boil. Cook and stir 2 minutes more. Remove from heat.
Stir in 2 tablespoons *butter* or *margarine* and ½ teaspoon finely shredded *lemon peel.* Gradually stir in ⅓ cup *lemon juice.* Mix well. Cover surface with clear plastic wrap. Cool the mixture to room temperature without stirring.

Café au Lait

Beignets
(see recipe, page 94)

Café au Lait

1 **cup ground coffee with chicory** 3 **cups water**	● Using coffee with chicory and water, prepare coffee according to coffee maker directions.
3 **cups light cream *or* milk**	● Meanwhile, heat the light cream or milk over low heat. Beat with rotary beater till foamy. Transfer cream to a warmed serving container. Stir coffee. Pour coffee and cream in equal amounts into serving cups. Makes 12 (4-ounce) servings.

Chicory makes dark, rich Louisiana coffee distinctive. But don't think of the green chicory leaves used in salads. The chicory that's mixed with coffee is actually a white, carrot-shape root. The root is sliced, dried, and roasted with a little oil before it's ground and added to the coffee.

Café Brûlot

3 **inches stick cinnamon, broken** 6 **whole cloves** 4 **sugar cubes** 1 **3x¼-inch strip orange peel, membrane removed** 1 **3x¼-inch strip lemon peel, membrane removed**	● In a blazer pan of a chafing dish combine cinnamon, cloves, sugar cubes, orange peel, and lemon peel.
½ **cup brandy** 2 **cups hot double-strength coffee**	● In a small saucepan heat brandy till nearly boiling. Remove from heat and ignite. Pour over mixture in blazer pan. Place blazer pan over chafing dish burner. Spoon brandy over sugar till cubes melt. Stir in coffee. Makes 4 (4-ounce) servings.

In the 1800s, special café brûlot bowls, ladles, and cups were traditional wedding presents for New Orleans brides.

Beignets

Pictured on page 92.

2¾ to 3¼ cups all-purpose
   flour
 1 package active dry yeast
 ½ teaspoon ground nutmeg
   (optional)
 1 cup milk
 ¼ cup sugar
 2 tablespoons shortening
 ½ teaspoon salt

● In a large mixer bowl stir together *1¼ cups* of the flour, yeast, and nutmeg, if desired. In a saucepan heat milk, sugar, shortening, and salt just till warm (115° to 120°) and the shortening is almost melted, stirring the mixture constantly.

Beignets (ben-YAE) are French fritters. Our light pillowy doughnuts are like those served in New Orleans, where Café au Lait (see recipe, page 93) is an essential accompaniment.

 1 egg

● Add the heated mixture to the flour mixture. Add egg. Beat with an electric mixer on low speed for ½ minute, scraping sides of bowl. Beat for 3 minutes on high speed. Using a spoon, stir in enough of the remaining flour to make a soft dough. Place dough in a greased bowl. Turn once to grease the surface. Cover bowl and refrigerate the dough overnight or till well chilled.

● Turn the dough out onto a lightly floured surface. Cover and let rest for 10 minutes. Roll into an 18x12-inch rectangle. Cut into thirty-six 3x2-inch rectangles. Cover and let rest for 30 minutes (dough will not be doubled).

   Shortening *or* cooking oil
      for deep-fat frying
   Powdered sugar

● In a large deep saucepan or deep-fat fryer heat 2 inches of melted shortening or cooking oil to 375°. Fry the dough rectangles, 2 or 3 at a time, about 1 minute or till golden, turning once. Drain on paper towels. Sift powdered sugar atop. Makes 36.

Index

A-B

Baked Cheese Grits, 58
Baked Flounder with
    Shrimp-and-Crab Stuffing, 20
Bananas Foster, 86
Beans
    Red Beans and Rice, 85
    White Bean Soup, 13
Beignets, 94
Beverages
    Café au Lait, 93
    Café Brûlot, 93
Blackened Redfish, 10
Boudin Blanc, 54
Bread Puddings
    Bread Pudding with Whiskey
        Sauce, 70
    Fruit Bread Pudding with
        Meringue Topping, 71

C

Café au Lait, 93
Café Brûlot, 93
Candied Yams, 62
Chicken
    Chicken and Okra Gumbo, 29
    Chicken and Tasso Jambalaya, 15
    Chicken, Oyster, and Sausage
        Gumbo, 25
    Fried Chicken, 51
Cocktail Sauce, 49
Coffee
    Café au Lait, 93
    Café Brûlot, 93
Courtbouillon, Redfish, 8
Crab
    Baked Flounder with
        Shrimp-and-Crab Stuffing, 20
    Crab Boil, 38
    Crab Boil Seasoning, 53
    Crab Chops, 18

Crab (continued)
    Fried Soft-Shell Crabs, 40
    Seafood Gumbo, 28
    Stuffed Crab, 17
Crawfish
    Crab Boil, 38
    Crawfish Boulettes, 42
    Crawfish Etouffée, 34
    Crawfish Pies, 32
    Crawfish Stew, 35

D-F

Dark Roux, 6
Desserts
    Bananas Foster, 86
    Bread Pudding with Whiskey
        Sauce, 70
    Doberge Cake, 90
    Fig Bars, 65
    Fruit Bread Pudding with
        Meringue Topping, 71
    Pecan Pie, 39
    Spiced Fig Cake, 79
    Sweet Potato-Molasses Pie, 72
    Syrup Cake, 65
Dirty Rice, 59
Doberge Cake, 90
Duck, Sausage-Stuffed, 19
Eggplant Dressing, 63
Figs
    Fig Bars, 65
    Fig Filling, 68
    Spiced Fig Cake, 79
Fish and Seafood
    Baked Flounder with
        Shrimp-and-Crab Stuffing, 20
    Blackened Redfish, 10
    Chicken, Oyster, and Sausage
        Gumbo, 25
    Crab Boil, 38
    Crab Chops, 18
    Crawfish Boulettes, 42
    Crawfish Etouffée, 34
    Crawfish Pies, 32
    Crawfish Stew, 35

Fish and Seafood (continued)
    Fried Frog Legs, 44
    Fried Seafood Platter, 48
    Fried Soft-Shell Crabs, 40
    Oysters Bienville, 82
    Pan-Fried Catfish, 46
    Pan-Fried Fish, 51
    Po' Boys, 88
    Redfish Courtbouillon, 8
    Sauce Piquante, 22
    Seafood Gumbo, 28
    Shrimp and Ham Jambalaya, 77
    Shrimp Creole, 88
    Shrimp Rémoulade, 84
    Stuffed Crab, 17
    Stuffed Mirlitons, 60
    Stuffed Peppers, 64
French Bread, 78
Fried Chicken, 51
Fried Frog Legs, 44
Fried Seafood Platter, 48
Fried Soft-Shell Crabs, 40
Fried Vegetables, 51
Frog Legs, Fried, 77
Fruit Bread Pudding with
    Meringue Topping, 71
Fry Coating, 51

G-H

Green Gumbo, 26
Grillades, 19
Grits, Baked Cheese, 58
Gumbos
    Chicken and Okra Gumbo, 29
    Chicken, Oyster, and Sausage
        Gumbo, 25
    Green Gumbo, 26
    Seafood Gumbo, 28
Ham
    Chicken and Tasso Jambalaya, 15
    Green Gumbo, 26
    Red Beans and Rice, 85
    Shrimp and Ham Jambalaya, 77
    White Bean Soup, 15
Hush Puppies, 43

J-O

Jambalayas
    Chicken and Tasso Jambalaya, 15
    Shrimp and Ham Jambalaya, 77
Jumbo Pralines, 69
King's Cake, 80
Lemon
    Doberge Cake, 90
    Lemon Filling, 90
    Lemon Icing, 90
    Sweet Dough Pies, 68
Les Orielles de Cochon, 67
Make-Ahead Roux, 6
Maque Choux, 56
Menus
    Crab Boil, 38
    Fais-Do-Do, 76
Mirlitons, Stuffed, 60
Okra, Smothered, 57
Oysters
    Chicken, Oyster, and Sausage
      Gumbo, 25
    Fried Seafood Platter, 48
    Oysters Bienville, 82
    Po' Boys, 88
    Stuffed Peppers, 64

P-R

Pan-Fried Catfish, 46
Pan-Fried Fish, 51
Party Relish Tray, 76
Pastry
    Pastry, 32
    Pastry for Single-Crust Pie, 39
Pecans
    Pecan Pie, 39
    Roasted Piquant Pecans, 59
Peppered Pork Chops, 23
Peppers, Stuffed, 64
Po' Boys, 88
Pork (see also Ham and Sausage)
    Boudin Blanc, 54
    Chicken and Tasso Jambalaya, 15
    Dirty Rice, 59

Pork (continued)
    Eggplant Dressing, 63
    Green Gumbo, 26
    Grillades, 19
    Peppered Pork Chops, 23
    Red Beans and Rice, 85
    Sauce Piquante, 22
    Shrimp and Ham Jambalaya, 77
    Stuffed Pork Roast, 12
    White Bean Soup, 15
Pot-Roasted Rabbit, 14
Praline Yam Casserole, 62
Rabbit, Pot-Roasted, 14
Red Beans and Rice, 85
Redfish Courtbouillon, 8
Rice, Dirty, 59
Roasted Piquant Pecans, 59
Rouxs
    Dark Roux, 6
    Make-Ahead Roux, 6
    Roux, 6

S

Sauces
    Cocktail Sauce, 49
    Sauce Piquante, 22
    Tartar Sauce, 49
    Whiskey Sauce, 70
Sausage
    Boudin Blanc, 54
    Chicken, Oyster, and
      Sausage Gumbo, 25
    Sausage-Stuffed Duck, 19
Seafood Gumbo, 28
Shrimp
    Baked Flounder with
      Shrimp-and-Crab Stuffing, 20
    Crawfish Boulettes, 42
    Crawfish Etouffée, 34
    Crawfish Pies, 32
    Crawfish Stew, 35
    Fried Seafood Platter, 48
    Seafood Gumbo, 28
    Shrimp and Ham Jambalaya, 77
    Shrimp Creole, 88
    Shrimp Rémoulade, 84

Smothered Okra, 57
Soups
    Turtle Soup, 89
    White Bean Soup, 13
Spiced Fig Cake, 79
Stuffed Crab, 17
Stuffed Mirlitons, 60
Stuffed Peppers, 64
Stuffed Pork Roast, 12
Stuffed Zucchini, 60
Sweet Dough Pies, 68
Sweet Potato-Molasses Pie, 72
Syrup Cake, 65

T-Z

Tartar Sauce, 49
Tasso Jambalaya, Chicken and, 15
Three-Pepper Seasoning, 53
Toasted Bread Crumbs, 60
Turtle Soup, 89
Vegetables, Fried, 51
Whiskey Sauce, 70
White Bean Soup, 13
Yams
    Candied Yams, 62
    Praline Yam Casserole, 62
Zucchini, Stuffed, 60

Tips

Fish Stock, 23
Fry It!, 44
Rice, Rice, Rice, 63
Shrimp Stock, 35
True Grits, 58